CRITICAL A
THE WORKS OF

The Last to Fall

"Authors Jim Rada and Richard Fulton have done an outstanding job of researching and chronicling this little-known story of those Marines in 1922, marking it as a significant moment in Marine Corps history."

- GySgt. Thomas Williams
Executive Director
U.S. Marine Corps Historical Company

Saving Shallmar

"But Saving Shallmar's Christmas story is a tale of compassion and charity, and the will to help fellow human beings not only survive, but also be ready to spring into action when a new opportunity presents itself. Bittersweet yet heartwarming, Saving Shallmar is a wonderful Christmas season story for readers of all ages and backgrounds, highly recommended."

Small Press Bookwatch

Battlefield Angels

"Rada describes women religious who selflessly performed life-saving work in often miserable conditions and thereby gained the admiration and respect of countless contemporaries. In so doing, Rada offers an appealing narrative and an entry point into the wealth of sources kept by the sisters."

Catholic News Service

Between Rail and River

"The book is an enjoyable, clean family read, with characters young and old for a broad-based appeal to both teens and adults. Between Rail and River also provides a unique, regional appeal, as it teaches about a particular group of people, ordinary working 'canawlers' in a story that goes beyond the usual coverage of life during the Civil War."

Historical Fiction Review

Canawlers

"A powerful, thoughtful and fascinating historical novel, Canawlers documents author James Rada, Jr. as a writer of considerable and deftly expressed storytelling talent."

Midwest Book Review

"James Rada, of Cumberland, has written a historical novel for high-schoolers and adults, which relates the adventures, hardships and ultimate tragedy of a family of boaters on the C&O Canal. ... The tale moves quickly and should hold the attention of readers looking for an imaginative adventure set on the canal at a critical time in history."

Along the Towpath

CLAY SOLDIERS

One Marine's Story of War, Art & Atomic Energy

Other books by James Rada, Jr.

Non-Fiction

Battlefield Angels: The Daughters of Charity Work as Civil War Nurses

Beyond the Battlefield: Stories from Gettysburg's Rich History

Echoes of War Drums: The Civil War in Mountain Maryland

The Last to Fall: The 1922 March, Battles & Deaths of U.S. Marines at Gettysburg

Looking Back: True Stories of Mountain Maryland

Looking Back II: More True Stories of Mountain Maryland

No North, No South: The Grand Reunion at the 50th Anniversary of the Battle of Gettysburg

Saving Shallmar: Christmas Spirit in a Coal Town

Fiction

Between Rail and River

Canawlers

Lock Ready

October Mourning

The Rain Man

CLAY SOLDIERS

One Marine's Story of War, Art & Atomic Energy

by

James Rada, Jr.

LEGACY PUBLISHING

A division of AIM Publishing Group

CLAY SOLDIERS

Published by Legacy Publishing, a division of AIM Publishing Group.
Gettysburg, Pennsylvania.

Printed in the United States of America.
First printing: April 2016.

ISBN 978-0692689875

Cover design by Grace Eyler.

LEGACY
PUBLISHING

315 Oak Lane • Gettysburg, Pennsylvania 17325

To Charles W. Caldwell,
a wonderful man who was willing to share
his life story with me.

CONTENTS

Pages from the autograph book that fourteen-year-old Chuck Caldwell took with him to the Seventy-Fifth Anniversary Reunion at Gettysburg in 1938. It contains nearly fifty autographs of Civil War veterans (on the left page) along with their ages, units, and hometowns. Chuck also has many photos of himself with the veterans (on the right page).

PREFACE

I thought that I was finished writing this book. It had been proofed and edited and sent out to my beta readers. Then one of my beta readers suggested that I should write a preface to explain why I chose to write about Chuck Caldwell and all of the places that life had taken him in his ninety-two year. It was a good idea since Chuck is not the typical subject for a biography.

Sure, he fought in World War II, but he wasn't a general. He was involved with atomic bomb testing, but he wasn't part of the brain trust that developed it. He's a talented artist, but not one of those artists whose works sell for obscene amounts of money.

Chuck is just a normal guy.

However, the life he has lived reminds me of that game called "Six Degrees of Kevin Bacon." Can you name anything or anyone else who connects the Civil War, WWII, atomic bomb testing, sculpting, the movie Gettysburg, the 1933 Chicago's World's Fair, and Walt Disney?

They all connect through Chuck Caldwell.

I first met him in 2014 when we sat down in his living room so I could start interviewing him for this book. He has a great memory, and what he can't remember, he has journals to help jump start his memories. He also has a great sense of humor and I enjoyed talking with him. I would visit every few weeks and sit down to talk for a couple hours. This went on for a year and a half. In between, I did a lot of research about what Chuck had told me.

With the seventy-fifth anniversary of WWII beginning this year, I believe it's important to remember the lives of the men and women of "the greatest generation." Of the more than sixteen million Americans who served in WWII, less than a million are still alive and even fewer still will be alive in 2020 when the WWII anniversary ends. How many great stories of that generation have been lost because no one took the time to record it or write it down?

As I said before, Chuck is an ordinary guy, but he has lived an extraordinary life. He pursued his dreams with focused determination, but he didn't let it keep him from having fun along the way or keep him from his family.

Here's hoping we can all be such ordinary people!

James Rada, Jr.
April 14, 2016

1938
THE LAST REUNION

Chuck Caldwell woke in the morning and wondered if he should cluck. The fourteen-year-old boy had spent the night sleeping in a chicken coop with his father. Not that the chickens were sharing the drafty wooden building with them. The roosts and nest boxes were empty, but the smell of feathers and feces hung in the air to remind him that clucking hens had once called the building home.

The chickens could have it back as far as Chuck was concerned. The low, wooden building with rows of wooden boxes mounted on three walls might be a fine home for chickens, but it hadn't been the most-comfortable place for Chuck to sleep. Throwing a mattress into a chicken coop hadn't turned it into a bedroom, either. Whenever Chuck had shifted on the thin mattress, he could feel the wire-mesh that served as a floor sink under him. If he looked over the edge of the mattress, he could stare through the mesh to the hard-packed earth outside that two feet below him. He actually hadn't minded the open floor too much. It had provided ventilation to keep it from getting too hot in the small building during the warm July night. The gentle draft from below also kept the unpleasant smells from becoming overwhelming. However, it had also allowed mosquitoes and other flying insects into the coop to disturb their sleep.

Chuck's mother and older sister would be glad that they hadn't come along on this trip. He didn't think that they all could have fit into the cramped eight-foot-by-eight-foot building, and Chuck couldn't imagine them sleeping here. When Barbara heard about this, his sister would probably start calling him some stupid name like "Chuck the Chicken" or "Cluck

Cluck Chuck." The taunts would be worth it, though. He and his father were here. He was in Gettysburg, Pennsylvania, where the tide of the Civil War had shifted.

The last day of June 1938, Chuck and his father had driven from their home in Orrville, Ohio, east along the Lincoln Highway. It was the first paved highway in the country and ran from New York to California. It made for a smooth ride in their Essex sedan, but it didn't make the 315-mile trip any shorter. They had traveled over the Appalachian Mountains, through small towns with interesting names like Freedom, Turtle Creek, and Ligonier, and the big city of Pittsburgh, which was 150 times larger than Orrville.

The drive had taken most of the day. They had stopped for food and gas along the way, but the breaks were as short as Chuck could make them. He urged his father on, and they arrived in Gettysburg late in the evening, although it was still daylight out. When the sedan parked along Chambersburg Street, both Chuck and his father were anxious to get out of the car. George Caldwell had needed to stretch his cramped body, but Chuck had wanted out because they were in Gettysburg. *The* Gettysburg.

It was a legendary, almost mythical, place to the young teenager. Gettysburg was a town that was forever stuck in its past because of its connection with the pivotal battle of the Civil War. It had been a town of around 2,000 residents in 1863 when more than 150,000 troops fought on the fields around the town and in the streets of Gettysburg. Chuck knew the names of the generals and officers who had fought here as well as he knew the names of his favorite baseball players. Lee. Meade. Chamberlain and so many others. Some were considered heroes, others villains, but they were all legends in Chuck's mind.

Seventy-five years after the famous battle, the population was around 5,800 and that's only if you counted permanent residents. In the summers, the population was at least double that as tourists visited the battlefield driving across the field where armies had once fought and thousands of soldiers died. Now hundreds of monuments had sprung up across the land like lonely sentinels to remind those visitors that they were on hallowed ground.

It wasn't the Caldwells first visit to Gettysburg. That had been two years earlier in 1936 when Chuck had been twelve years old. That summer, the entire Caldwell Family, including Chuck's mother, Ellen, and sister, Barbara, had arrived in Gettysburg for a family vacation. For Chuck, it had been a dream come true. There'd been no chicken coop for a bedroom then. The family had stayed at a tourist court in town and had hired a guide to lead them in a tour of the Gettysburg battlefield.

During the driving tour of the battlefield, Chuck marveled at the open, green fields interrupted occasionally with large stone monuments. He would have stopped at every gray stone monument if he had been able to in order to read what had been inscribed in stone.

The largest of the monuments was the 110-foot-tall Pennsylvania State Memorial. It commemorated the 34,530 Pennsylvania soldiers who had fought at Gettysburg, and it had been dedicated just in time for the last great reunion at Gettysburg in 1913. The 100-foot-square pedestal made from North Carolina granite had four corner towers connected by arches that supported a dome and observation deck. The deck could be reached by a spiral staircase in the tower. Besides the panels with soldiers' names, the walls also hold bas-relief sculptures. The memorial contained more than 1,400 tons of broken stone, more than 1,250 tons of granite, 740 tons of sand, more than 360 tons of cement, fifty tons of steel bars and twenty-two tons of marble.

Chuck had climbed one of the staircases in the towers to reach the observation deck. From the top of the monument, he had a commanding 360-degree view of the battlefield. He could see miles in any direction. He imagined soldiers dressed in blue or gray on foot and on horseback charging and firing rifles at each other. He looked at the tree lines, searching for cannons.

For most of the tour, the guide sat in the front of the old Essex describing how the three-day battle in 1863 had progressed.

"As we would drive by the Peach Orchard, he'd tell us about it and then say, 'And the fighting was mighty, mighty severe.' Then we'd drive by the Wheatfield and he would tell us about what happened there and then say, 'And the fighting was mighty, mighty severe," Chuck recalled.

By the time the Caldwells reached their third or fourth stop on the tour where "the fighting was mighty, mighty severe", Chuck and his sister were hiding their faces behind their hands, giggling and trying not to laugh out loud from the backseat of the car.

When the Caldwells finished their vacation in Gettysburg, they drove further east through York, Pennsylvania, which had served as the national capital in 1777 when the British drove the politicians from Philadelphia, and then through the heart of Amish country in Lancaster County. They finally stopped at Valley Forge. Oddly enough, the Revolutionary War site where General George Washington's Continental Army had encamped for the winter and suffered through starvation, disease, and malnutrition brought back memories of Chuck's paper route in Orrville.

Chuck delivered the *Courier-Crescent*, Orrville's twice-weekly newspaper, tossing papers to front stoops as he pedaled his bicycle through his hometown. On one section of his route, though, he had to dismount his bike and hike up a steep hill past the Crown Hill Cemetery at the intersection of Crown Hill Road and West High Street.

"On winter days, I was always imagining myself at Valley

Forge, climbing up this hill in the deep snow and then having the person I was going to see not pay me for the week," Chuck recalled.

He enjoyed the visit to Valley Forge, but it was the Civil War and the Battle of Gettysburg that stuck in his memory. Part of the reason for his interest in history, and in particular, the Civil War, was that his great-grandfather had fought in the war.

Chuck didn't know it at the time, but Private Isaac Caldwell had served in the First Tennessee Volunteers as part of Archer's Brigade. A Union cavalry officer is believed to have fired the first shot in the Battle of Gettysburg at 7:30 a.m. on July 1, 1863, when the Confederate Army was still three miles west of Gettysburg. The Confederate Army halted and sent out skirmishers. Confederate General James Archer's brigade encountered little resistance at first. Union infantry flanked Archer and caught him by surprise. The Confederates started a retreat through the woods and across Willoughby Run, but Archer and 300 of his men were surrounded and captured. Private Caldwell's company had marched near the front of the Confederate Army as it approached Gettysburg. Isaac was also one of the early casualties in the battle when he was wounded at Willoughby Run. He had survived the battle and the war, though, unlike thousands of other men.

In the 1930s, those whom the Civil War had not taken were slowly being picked off by time. Isaac Caldwell had died in 1885, By 1938, only an estimated 8,000 Civil War veterans were still alive out of the more than 3.2 million men who had served in the armed forces. Chuck wished that he could have met all of them. He certainly gave it his best effort, but there was only so much that a fourteen-year old could do.

His father, George, who was the pastor at the Orrville Presbyterian Church, often spoke at other churches or at meetings of pastors that were held outside of Orrville. Whenever he did,

George would pour through the local newspapers and ask about whether there were any Civil War veterans living in the towns he visited. If there were, George would call them and make an appointment to stop by and get a picture, autograph, and some biographical information about them. Then he would give Chuck the mementos when he returned home.

Family members who knew of Chuck's interest would save stories about Civil War veterans that popped up in their hometown newspapers from time to time. They would clip them carefully and mail them off to Chuck. He would open the envelopes like they were Christmas presents and read the stories looking for new information and names. Then he would paste the clippings into a scrapbook.

Chuck would often write to the veterans whose addresses he could find. He would pepper them with questions about their service in the Civil War, the battles they had fought, the hardships they had endured, and the training they had received. A good number of the veterans wrote him back. Chuck corresponded with some of them right up until they died.

With the seventy-fifth anniversary of the Civil War beginning in 1936, many newspapers started running features about the veterans who lived in their circulation areas. The articles allowed the veterans to recount their war-time experiences. Chuck had read as many of the articles as he could find so he had been overjoyed to find out that he and his father would be traveling to Gettysburg for the last, great anniversary.

Most of the veterans had arrived earlier the same day that Chuck and his father had arrived, but they came to Gettysburg on twelve special Pullman trains. Some of the men were so frail that they had to be carried off of the trains on stretchers.

The Gettysburg that the Caldwells drove into in 1938 was a much larger town than the Gettysburg of two years prior. Not larger in terms of size, but it had many more people crammed into that space. Cars crept along the roads, bumper to bumper.

Tents were pitched in open fields forming small communities. People clustered tightly on sidewalks, reminding Chuck of pictures he had seen of big cities like New York and Philadelphia. Many of the people on the sidewalks were probably from those cities and thinking about how uncrowded Gettysburg was.

Because of the expected crowds, the borough had worked to make a good impression on visitors and veterans alike. In the weeks leading up to the reunion, workmen had repaired all of the streets leading into Gettysburg and removed any weeds along the sidewalks. Flags were draped across the streets—Chambersburg, York, Baltimore, and Carlisle—leading from the town square. Business windows were filled with displays about the anniversary. Public buildings were festooned with flags. The borough had even arranged for many of the buildings to receive a fresh coat of paint. At night, the town was lit up with red, white, and blue lights.

The *Gettysburg Times* reported, "Gettysburg will present its brightest and gayest appearance in 25 years." One Confederate veteran's wife said all of the activity and decorations in town reminded her of a huge street carnival.

Tim Murphy of Harrisburg was a big reason for this declaration. Murphy had worked in event promotion and decorating for more than twenty-five years. He had learned showmanship from working with the Barnum and Bailey's Circus and Buffalo Bill's Wild West Show. He had also decorated Washington, D.C. for the inaugurations of Franklin D. Roosevelt, Calvin Coolidge, and Warren G. Harding. Perhaps most importantly, he had helped decorate Gettysburg for the Grand Reunion of 1913 when 57,000 Civil War veterans had come to Gettysburg to remember the battle and their days in the Blue or the Gray. Chuck's head swung back and forth anxiously looking for Civil War veterans in the crowd, but he didn't see anyone whom he could point to and say, "I want to meet him!" Most of the men wore nice suits, though some of them had forsaken their jackets because of the heat. They were far too young to have served in the Civil War. Chuck did see some men in brown uniforms, but they were modern soldiers.

While the Caldwells hadn't needed to make a room reservation two years ago, this year, each innkeeper, tourist court owner, and motel manager with whom they inquired told them the same thing. They had arrived too late in the day. All of their rooms were filled. Try back around lunch time tomorrow.

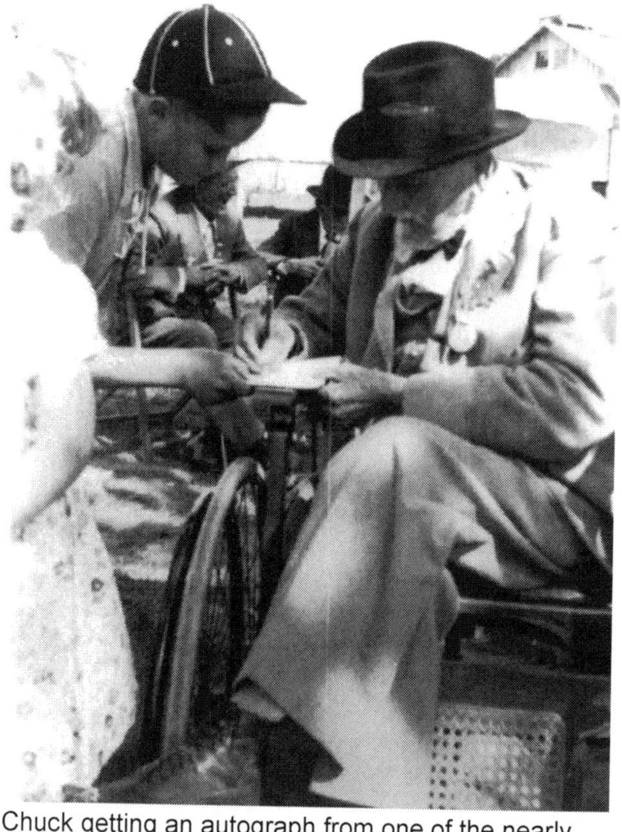

Chuck getting an autograph from one of the nearly 2,000 Civil War veterans who attended the seventy-fifth anniversary of the Battle of Gettysburg in 1938. Courtesy of Chuck Caldwell.

With each rejection, it looked like it was less likely that Chuck and his father would find a place to stay for the night at least in Gettysburg. Both of them dreaded getting back in the car to drive on to Biglerville, New Oxford, or Emmitsburg in search of a room.

A farmer saved the day for them. George Caldwell started talking to the man on the street, hoping to get a lead as to where he could find a room in town. The farmer agreed with everyone else that all of the rooms were filled with tourists visiting for the seventy-fifth anniversary of the battle. Then he offered the Caldwells the use of his old chicken coop, which was currently vacant.

That was why Chuck found himself waking up in a chicken coop on July 1, 1938, rather than a bed. He shook his father awake and they washed up in the farmer's house, changed clothes and drove back into Gettysburg.

One night in a chicken coop had been enough for the Caldwells. George made sure that he took part of the afternoon to revisit the tourist camps and hotels in town until they found a place to stay that offered them a real bed without any ventilation through the floor.

The Civil War veterans weren't staying in hotels or inns, either. Even though their rooms were tents, they were five-star accommodations compared to a chicken coop.

The veterans' camp had been constructed on the north end of Gettysburg College and also on some adjacent privately owned property. The Pennsylvania Blue and Gray Planning Commission had decided to house the veterans in tents just as had been done during the 1913 reunion when more than 6,500 tents had been erected in a temporary camp south of Gettysburg. Although far fewer veterans attended the seventy-fifth anniversary reunion, there simply wasn't enough room for all of them in hotels and constructing wooden barracks would have been too costly.

Planning for the seventy-fifth anniversary reunion had begun in 1935, but men of the Civilian Conservation Corps hadn't started construction of the camp until April 26, 1938. Leonard Shealer, one the workers who helped build the camp, hauled wood to build the camp boardwalks and tent frames. Once the reunion activities began, Shealer hauled garbage from the kitchen in his truck and also slept there.

Boardwalk streets were laid out in a grid fashion. Union veteran tents were located on lettered streets from Biglerville Road to Mummasburg Road. Confederate veteran tents lined numbered streets from Mummasburg Road to the Reading Railroad. The Confederate and Union sections of the camp were split by Mummasburg Road.

Each veteran was given either a United States flag or a Confederate flag to display in front of his tent if he wanted to do so. Annette Tucker, wife of a Confederate veteran at the reunion, wrote, "At the time I felt so loyal to the Government for making this meeting possible and for all the favors they were bestowing upon us that it didn't seem proper to display the Confederate flag, not even at the Reunion, even if we were permitted this privilege, so I folded mine to bring home for a souvenir and perhaps use at our own U. D. C. meetings."

Short wooden walks ran off the streets at right angles leading to the nine-foot by nine-foot tents. Each tent had two cots; one for the veteran and one for his attendant. The tents had wash stands and electric lights in them. They also had rain flys in front of them that offered shade so that the veteran could sit outside and talk to his neighbors or greet passersby by like Chuck.

"It was a thrill to be able to see both armies together at one time. It was just too much. I would have walked from home to be there," Chuck said.

Fourteen-year-old Chuck Caldwell poses for a picture with Confederate veteran Stephen Howe in Gettysburg in 1938. Courtesy of Chuck Caldwell.

The men Chuck saw seemed frail in comparison to the soldiers they had been in their youth. Now in their nineties and even their hundreds, their hair, if they still had any, was white along with their sideburns, mustaches, and goatees. Many of them could stand for only short stretches and spent most of their time sitting in wheelchairs supplied by the reunion commission.

Nearly all of them dressed in coats, vests, and neckties. Here and there, one of the veterans would dress in a shabby military uniform that was seventy-five years old. This was their special reunion and their time in the national spotlight. They wanted to make a good first impression with people they met.

For some, Gettysburg held such a special place in their hearts and minds that they wanted to die on the battlefield. William W. Banks, a veteran who served with Company H, Eighteenth Alabama Infantry, sent the Quartermaster General of the United States a telegram saying that he represented a group of veterans "do desire to remain here on this hallowed hill till Gabriel shall call us to that eternal party where there is no strife, bitter hate, nor bloodshed and we are one for all and all for one."

Because of his father's efforts to help Chuck meet living Civil War veterans, Chuck had actually met some of these men before, especially if they lived fairly close to Orrville. While those meetings stuck out in his young memory, the veterans rarely remembered meeting one particular young boy for a few minutes.

"They were close to 100 years old," Chuck said. "They wouldn't remember a little kid."

One young attendee named John Stonesifer remembered the veterans as being grumpy without much to say.

That didn't stop Chuck from approaching each veteran whom he could find. He carried his Brownie camera and an autograph book and looked more like a cub reporter than a tourist.

He would introduce himself and ask the veteran to sign his name and write the outfit that he had served in during the war and his hometown. Chuck also asked his father to take a picture of the veteran and Chuck. The brown-haired and brown-eyed Chuck looks very young in the pictures standing around five feet tall and as thin as a rail. He would be asking the veteran any questions he could think of whether it was about a particular battle, military life, or their life after the war.

One of the men whom Chuck met was John C. Smith of Meridian, Mississippi. The 108-year-old veteran had fought with the Forty-Sixth Georgia as the Confederates charged Little Roundtop at Gettysburg.

"Somewhere in that furious charge across the valley, a spent bullet thudded into Smith's cheek and he spit it out into his powder-blackened hand and went on to fight across the hill top and, finally, to give up to the Union reinforcements," *The Daily Herald* (Circleville, Ohio) reported.

Chuck was enraptured with the stories the veterans told him and he could have listened to them for days on end. However, his camp tour was somewhat hampered by rain in the late afternoon and evening of Friday, July 1. Though the rainfall kept the temperature down, it also sent many people indoors. When the rain started, the camp headquarters sent a truckload of umbrellas to the veterans' camp. More than 2,000 umbrellas were distributed to veterans so they could continue touring the town in buses that were also provided by the camp headquarters.

One of the first veterans whom Chuck met during the reunion was ninety-one-year-old Henry Rogers of Santa Monica, California. Rogers showed off his patriotism during one of the bus tours on the battlefield when he stood up and recited Lincoln's Gettysburg Address to the cheers of the other riders on the bus who were nearly all Civil War veterans themselves.

Rogers had served as a dispatch orderly with the Fortieth Illinois Infantry during the war. Three of his brothers had also served in the same company. During the Battle of Kenesaw Mountain in Georgia on June 27, 1864, Rogers and his brothers had charged against a regiment in which their uncle was a soldier.

Rogers' wife, Elizabeth, had accompanied her husband to the reunion and served as his attendant. She was seventy-eight years old, but still in good enough health to take care of her husband and serving as his attendant allowed them to share the same tent in the veterans' camp. Chuck struck up an acquaintance with Rogers and corresponded with the aged veteran until he died on November 20, 1938.

The big feature of July 1 was the opening ceremony at the Gettysburg College Stadium at 2 p.m. featuring U.S. Secretary of War Harry H. Woodring as the main speaker. One of the other speakers during the ceremony was the Reverend John M. Claypool of St. Louis, another one of the veterans whom Chuck met and had sign his autograph book. Claypool was the commander of the United Confederate Veterans and a descendant of John Hancock.

Claypool's remarks were broadcast over national radio. He good-naturedly noted that if the South hadn't surrendered in 1865, it would have continued fighting using guerilla warfare still today, but Southerners had been too high-minded to continue fighting a lost cause.

"We can't hold anything against each other," Claypool said. "I speak as the representative of real Americans and as a real American myself. God bless you all."

That second night in Gettysburg, Chuck and his father slept in a bed in a room in a tourist camp, but Chuck was awake early in the morning ready to go visiting the veterans' camp. Many of the tents were empty as their occupants were out touring the battlefield. Among the tents that were occupied, Chuck often found the aged veterans sleeping.

He and his father toured the Union camp first and then crossed the street to the Confederate camp.

"I could hardly wait to get to the Confederate camp because there were so many fewer of them," Chuck recalls.

During one of his trips to the Confederate camp, young Chuck met O. Richard Gillette, who had served in Davis's Brigade with the Second Mississippi. Though he fought in a number of major battles during the war, the only time that he was wounded was at the Battle of Antietam.

"A piece of shrapnel hit me in the knee. It didn't hurt me much, but the worst of it was it ruined my britches," Gillette told the *Gettysburg Times*.

The old veteran had lived next-door to Jefferson Davis. Gillette had joined the army when he was fifteen years old. Besides being near where the Confederate troops had pierced the Union line during Pickett's Charge, he had also seen Confederate General Stonewall Jackson mortally wounded during the Battle of Chancellorsville in 1863.

Chuck had his picture taken with the man. Gillette still had his hair, though it was white and thinning. He also had a thick white mustache. Chuck asked him to sign his autograph book. Gillette wrote in it that he had been at the opening and close of the Battle of Gettysburg.

Gillette invited the Caldwells into his tent and out of the sun. He sat down on his cot and reached a hand under it. He pulled out a stone jug filled with whiskey.

"Would you like a drink?" Gillette offered George Caldwell.

George shook his head. "No, thank you."

Gillette shrugged and poured himself a glass and sipped it. Then the trio began to talk with Chuck anxious to ask questions about the war of the weathered veteran. In an old newsreel from the reunion, an interviewer has a conversation with Gillette, which more than likely resembled Chuck's and dozens of others Gillette had during the reunion.

"General Gillette, will you tell us in your own words your experiences during the celebrated Pickett Charge at the Bloody Angle at the Battle of Gettysburg?" the interviewer asks.

"Well, I belonged to the Davis Division, that Davis Brigade and we get about ten feet at the slope, then we had to turn. Those that were living had to turn," Gillette replies.

"What do you mean by *turn*?"

"Run, run like hell."

"You don't mean to say, General Gillette, that soldiers run?"

"Well, if one tells you he didn't, he's telling you a damn lie."

Later in the day, Chuck and his father watched the thirty-unit parade through Gettysburg that ended at the stadium where the Civil War veterans reviewed the modern military men and their equipment. The parade included drum and bugle corps representing the major veteran organizations in the country and many of the states that had troops at the Battle of Gettysburg. Interspersed between the drum and bugle corps were regular army units representing infantry, tanks, anti-aircraft, field artillery and cavalry. The other armed forces also had units in the parade. With all of the men and equipment, the parade stretched out for three miles between the reviewing stand at the college and the intersection of Baltimore Pike and Emmitsburg Road. It took two-and-a-half hours for everything in the parade to pass.

The next day was the Caldwells' last full day in Gettysburg. Chuck once again spent time walking through the camps looking for veterans with whom to speak. By the end of the day, he would have nearly fifty autographs from Civil War veterans in his book along with their basic information and picture.

During the afternoon, veterans shook hands across the stone wall at The Angle. The same thing had been done at the fiftieth anniversary reunion in 1913, and one couldn't help but notice that there were far fewer veterans around to participate in it in 1938.

The big event of July 3 was the dedication of the Peace Memorial with its eternal flame, which stood on the hill northwest of the veterans' camp.

President Franklin D. Roosevelt arrived by train at a temporary platform next to the Confederate camp and was escorted in a car to the memorial where more than 200,000 people waited.

Chuck and his father were in the crowd not too far away from the memorial. The weather was hot, feeling even more so because of the tightly packed bodies. Many people stood for hours waiting to hear the president speak, and at least a half dozen people had to be carried away to get medical care after they collapsed from heat exhaustion.

Chuck Caldwell's view of the Peace Light dedication ceremony at Gettysburg in 1938. Courtesy of Chuck Caldwell.

The president spoke less than ten minutes. Among his comments he noted, "In later years, new needs arose and with them new tasks, world-wide in their perplexities, their bitterness and their modes of strife. Here in our land we give thanks that, avoiding war, we seek our ends through the peaceful processes of popular government under the Constitution." He concluded his remarks by accepting the monument on behalf of federal government "in the spirit of brotherhood and peace."

"The Star-Spangled Banner" started playing. Two ropes reached to the top of the monument and were hidden within a fifty-foot-long American flag. The ropes were pulled and the flag slowly came down to be caught by Union veteran George N. Lockwood, Confederate veteran A. G. Harris, and two regular army attendants. Lockwood was a ninety-two-year-old Union veteran from Los Angeles and Harris was ninety-one-year-old Confederate veteran from McDonough, Georgia. Both men wore the uniforms of their respective armies as they performed their solemn duty.

Following the dedication, the U.S. Army staged a simulated air raid on Gettysburg that included forty-eight aircraft from light attack planes to large bombers. Searchlights on the ground were directed up at the planes as they dropped flares.

The military demonstration continued with tank maneuvers by the Sixty-Sixth Infantry Provisional Tank Battalion near Glatfelter Hall on the Gettysburg College campus.

Once night fell, fireworks were launched from the crest of Oak Hill.

Chuck fell asleep that night exhausted, but he knew that over the past three days he had seen something special and he had been a part of history. That was what he wanted in life.

1930-1941
ORRVILLE

Although Charles Warner Caldwell had been born in Princeton, Illinois, on November, 26, 1923, Chuck didn't remember the state of his birth except for when he visited his mother's side of the family who still lived there. His father's work as a minister took the family from congregation to congregation, and the Caldwells moved to Missouri about a month after Chuck was born.

The Caldwells lived in Cameron, Missouri, for nearly five years. It is a small town in the northwestern corner of the state with a population of around 3,300. Some of Chuck's earliest childhood memories were from that town.

"That's where I learned to curse," he said with a grin and a chuckle.

A couple of neighborhood boys about Chuck's age apparently came from a family that used coarser language than the Caldwells spoke. Chuck quickly learned that such words weren't acceptable in his Christian home. They left a bad taste of soap in his mouth.

As Chuck neared six years old, his family moved to Penney Farms, Florida, in 1928.

James Cash Penney was a Missourian whose father had been a poor farmer and a part-time Baptist preacher. The elder Penney father raised his son to be a strong Christian and have an equally strong work ethic.

When Penney moved to Colorado in 1898, he began working in a dry goods store and found that the work suited him. Guy Johnson and Thomas Callahan owned the chain of stores called "The Golden Rule." They followed this rule and rewarded Penney's hard work and innovative management and marketing style by offering to make him a partner.

Penney accepted and began managing and opening new The Golden Rule Stores over the next few years. In 1907, Johnson and Callahan sold their interest in the business to Penney. Penney incorporated his company as the J. C. Penney Company in 1913. He then phased out The Golden Rule name and expanded the J.C. Penney Stores nationwide.

Never forgetting his roots, Penney opened a 120,000-acre experimental farm community in Florida in 1926. His idea was to give farmers who were down on their luck a place to work and re-establish themselves until they reached a point where they could buy their own farms. The plan was a bit too grand, though, and it was eventually scaled back to become a community for retired ministers of all faiths called Penney Farms.

Chuck's father, George, was the community's first paid minister. It must have been an intimidating calling for him. Rather than preaching to the choir, he was taking it even further and preaching to the ministers; many of whom had more experience behind the pulpit than George. One of those preachers was Charles Caldwell, George's father and a retired preacher.

With both a father and grandfather who were clergy, it might have been expected that Chuck would follow in his family's calling. Chuck never showed an interest in going that route, though. In fact, it was hard keeping him still enough during a service to even listen to the sermon.

"I was a pew climber in church," Chuck said. "I just wouldn't sit still."

With George preaching at the front of the church, it fell to Ellen Caldwell to keep her ears open to the sermon and her eyes on young Chuck as he would crawl over, under, and across the pews disturbing nearby churchgoers.

His mother finally stopped trying to pull Chuck off of the

pews to make him sit down. It was like trying to hold onto water. Instead, Ellen Caldwell gave her son paper and a pencil and let him draw hoping to focus his attention elsewhere.

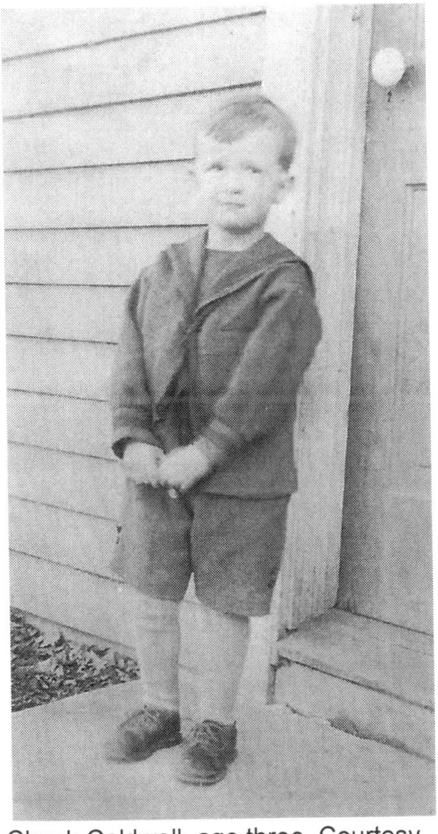

Chuck Caldwell, age three. Courtesy of Chuck Caldwell.

It worked. Chuck became so focused on creating something on the sheet of paper that the only part of him moving during the service was his hand. He still wasn't listening to the sermons, but at least he wasn't disturbing everyone around him.

This soon led to another problem that needed solving, though.

"I was not a smart kid," Chuck said. "I would draw a car on

the paper, looking the way it should with four wheels and everything. Then when I got home, I couldn't figure out why it wouldn't stand up."

Ellen's solution to Chuck's problem was to give her son a piece of colored modeling clay. He could shape this into a car and it would stand up. Then if he wanted it to be something else, he could reshape it into a boat or a car or a soldier. His only limits were his imagination and the amount of clay that he had.

"When people found out that I liked clay, they were like 'Well, it's only ten cents!' and that's all I got for gifts from then on. I didn't mind that because it was what I wanted," Chuck said. And, as it turned out, Chuck needed lots of clay for his many sculptures.

He started school in Penney Farms in 1929, but as you can imagine, a retirement community with only ninety-eight cottages had few children that needed educating. The school had four rooms and less than two dozen students. Chuck had been only one of two children in his first-grade class. Multiple grades were condensed into a single class, but Chuck still longed for a friend his own age.

By the beginning of the next school year, the Caldwells had moved to Orrville, Ohio. It was a small town about twenty-six miles west of Canton, Ohio. Like many small towns its size, it had a healthy business district along Main Street through the center of the town. Most the buildings were brick structures built in the late 1800s and early 1900s.

George had accepted the position as reverend for the First Presbyterian Church right in the heart of Orrville at the corner of North Main and East Church streets. The church was also the only Presbyterian Church in the town and had been there since a year after Orrville had been established. Many of the town fathers had been Presbyterian, including the Orrs, for whom the town was named.

The Caldwells lived in a three-bedroom house on East Paradise Street. Chuck thought that was an excellent name for a street on which a minister lived. The house had two floors, an attic, and a basement. The main floor had a long sunporch on the front of it. Chuck soon took over a section of it for his work area for creating his clay sculptures.

The main floor also had a living room, dining room, sewing area for his mother, and a kitchen with a small side porch.

"I remember the big excitement in the house when we got a refrigerator," Chuck said. "It meant no more signs in the window saying we needed twenty-five pounds of ice for the ice box."

Chuck enjoyed his new home as did the rest of his family. George Caldwell was preaching to his congregation, giving history talks to school groups, and involving himself with the business community.

Ellen was a registered nurse. She had worked a little in Florida, but her children were still young and she hadn't wanted to leave them in someone else's care. In Orrville, she still made sure to be home with her children as much as she could, but she began assisting doctors on their house calls, particularly if the patient was a maternity patient.

Orrville, as an incorporated town, was not yet seventy years old when the Caldwells moved there in 1930. It was the place they would call home for the rest of Chuck's childhood.

The first settlers had arrived in the area in 1814 when James Taggart staked out a quarter section due him as a Revolutionary War veteran. The early families in the region were Irish, Pennsylvania Dutch, and German, but as the country grew and the railroads passed into the region, new names and faces helped grow the community into a town that incorporated in 1864.

Orrville was a rail town with the Pennsylvania Railroad and

the Cleveland, Akron, and Columbus Railroad running through it. That meant like most rail towns, the buildings were perpetually dingy from soot and cinders coming from the train stacks as the trains passed through the town or waited at Union Station. Wives washed their windows at least once a week and husbands used water hoses and long-handled brushes to scrub the outside walls of their homes free of soot.

The Caldwells in their home in Orrville, Ohio. Left to right: Ellen, George, Barbara, and Chuck. Courtesy of Chuck Caldwell.

Those railroads were the reason the town had grown. They brought people into Orrville every day. Others moved into the town from the surrounding farms. Wayne County was a rural county with only three towns of any size; Wooster, Orrville, and Rittman. Orrville also had the J. M. Smucker's Company. Jerome Smucker had owned a small pressed cider mill near Mill Street in 1897. "Wanting something to sell after the cider season, Jerome used a recipe learned as a boy and produced apple butter-almost 1000 gallons the first year," Bob Witmer wrote in *Orrville, Ohio Historical Walking Guide.* The apple butter was a success and by 1923 the J. M. Smucker Company had started manufacturing jellies and preserves for national distribution.

Orrville seemed like a metropolis compared to Penney Farms, at least to Chuck. His parents could remember truly huge cities like Chicago, but Chuck was only seven years old and Orrville with nearly 4,500 people was larger than Penney Farms by a factor of twenty.

What he liked best was that it meant that many of those 4,500 people were kids and a lot of them were his age. In fact, there were so many children in town that a second grade school had to be built in 1908 to handle the overcrowding at Walnut Street School and then a third school in 1913. Chuck attended Oak Street School, which had four rooms on two floors and dozens of children in grades one through six.

Orrville was not a small town, but not a city either. It was just the right size for a young boy to explore without too much adult supervision.

Chuck liked growing up in Orrville. The people were friendly and he could find plenty of things to keep him occupied. Orrville had lots of places a young boy could explore from the woods behind his home to the train yards to ice skating on the mill pond.

Chuck and his friends liked to play at Griffith's Pond at

the end of East Paradise Street. It was a shallow pond, but deep enough for swimming and fishing. When the pond froze in the winter, the ice was cut and sold to families to be used in ice boxes. The boys built a raft from scrap lumber they collected and were surprised and delighted when it actually floated on the pond. They grabbed long sticks to serve as swords and boarded the newly launched pirate ship and set sail to plunder imaginary merchant vessels whose holds were filled with gold.

One of Chuck's friends, Rex Zimmerman, lived on the other side of Paradise Street across from the swamp. When the boys weren't pretending to be pirates, they might be found at Rex's house setting up large-scale battles with all of Rex's lead soldiers, which was the common material for toy soldiers until after World War II. Chuck could have made his own soldiers, but clay wouldn't have held up to the wear and tear that boys placed on their soldiers during their mock battles.

On Saturdays during the summer, the boys spent a lot of time playing baseball on the baseball diamond maintained by the Orrville National Bank. Chuck was not a natural athlete, but he enjoyed playing the game.

He also enjoyed watching the Orrville High School Red Rider football team play. Chuck was already a fan of the University of Alabama Crimson Tide at this point, but in the days before television, he couldn't see them play so he settled for the next best thing. He rooted for his home team and kept careful stats on how well they played.

Chuck wasn't the only football enthusiast in Orrville. "In 1934, students were so elated after defeating Wooster that they broke out of school during a pep rally and marched to downtown Orrville, halting traffic and snake-dancing in the street. They went to Wooster and also blocked the street, quickly bringing police action," Witmer wrote.

The Red Riders played on a field on North Mill behind the Smucker's plant that had night lighting. Although the field served its purpose, games were occasionally interrupted when thick, acrid smoke from the nearby onion fields invaded games and forced people to leave. At other times, fans had to deal with the smell of dead animals from Bechtol's Slaughter House and other odors from Cottage Creamery, Quality Castings, or Smucker's.

It was hard for Chuck to get in trouble as he and his friends explored Orrville and enjoyed the types of things that caught the attention of a young boy. Not that he or any boys his age considered it trouble. To them, it was simply having some fun catching a snake that happened to be poisonous, using unbroken windows in old buildings to improve their pitching aim, or climbing a tree as far up as they could before the branches could no longer hold their weight. They didn't consider it dangerous, but plenty of adults thought otherwise and always seemed to be around to stop a boy from having fun.

Maybe, the adults were a bit overcautious, but many of them still remembered when four-year-old Melvin Horst disappeared without a trace in 1928 less than a block from his home near Vine Street and Paradise Street. Melvin had been playing with friends on a vacant lot on Chestnut Street within earshot of his mother's call. However, when his mother called for him at 4:30 p.m. on December 27, he never showed up. His friends said that he had left earlier, carrying a red toy truck that he had received as a Christmas present. He was last seen south of the Orrville Leather Company several blocks away from his home. The search lasted for weeks and moved from door-to-door searches to looking for the youngster outside of the Orrville town limits. No sign of Melvin was ever found. No ransom demand was ever made. Accusations went back and forth as rumors spread not only throughout Orrville, but across the nation. Backyards were excavated in search of a body, but nothing was ever found and no one was ever charged with kidnapping or worse. In one instance, Hanna and Earl Conrad accused each other of murdering the boy until police dug up their backyard and found nothing.

People still remembered that time, and the adults still watched out for children not wanting to have another Melvin Horst disappear.

The Caldwells' home on East Paradise Street in Orrville, Ohio. Courtesy of Chuck Caldwell.

A year after the Caldwells moved into their home on East Paradise Street, George's parents were coming up from Penney Farms to visit when Chuck's grandmother, Laura Caldwell, who was seventy years old at the time, took sick. She died from a heart condition shortly after she and Charles arrived in Orrville. Her family buried her in the Crown Hill Cemetery in Orrville, giving the Caldwells an even stronger connection to the town.

When Charles returned to Florida after the funeral, it was as a single man for the first time in forty years. Thirteen months later, Chuck and his family traveled to Detroit to see Chuck's grandfather wed Alma Hubbard.

Alma had been a widow for longer than Charles and she had grown twin daughters from her previous marriage. However, she was nearly thirty years younger than Charles. As it turned out, Alma was also Ellen Caldwell's older sister.

"It was real weird," Chuck said, "because my cousins were now also my aunts."

If George had any concerns about his father marrying his sister-in-law, he must have put them aside. He performed the marriage ceremony in Alma's Detroit home on September 1, 1932.

The 1933 Chicago World's Fair was called "A Century of Progress" to celebrate Chicago's centennial since its incorporation in 1833. Chicago was a six-hour drive from Orrville, but the World's Fair was a big enough event not to be missed and worth a day of driving.

The Caldwells made the road trip to Chicago to visit the fair during the summer when Chuck and Barbara were out of school. Ellen had two brothers living in the city so they had a place to stay and wouldn't have to worry about finding a room in a city crowded with tourists from all over the world.

At ten years old, Chuck had become an avid collector of baseball cards. Any time he found himself with a penny, he would stop at the grocery store that he passed on his way to school and purchase a single baseball card with his penny. His favorite team was the Cleveland Indians. Since Cleveland was about sixty miles north of Orrville, he and his father had gone to a couple of the Indians' home games. Chuck anxiously looked for players' cards, but the Indians were sorely underrepresented in the set produced by the Goudey Gum Company. While a star player like Babe Ruth might have four cards in the set, the entire Indians team only had nine players represented, each with an individual card.

It made finding those Indians' cards that much more special for Chuck. He searched for Napoleon Lajoie, Earl Averill, and George Connally among the cards and was delighted when he found one.

He carried his cards with him in a shoebox everywhere he went. As with many a young man, they were his treasure. He had them with him on the trip to Chicago, but he left the box in the car the first night in town. When he came out of his Uncle Leo Hawk's home the next morning, he found that the car had been broken into. The cards that he had worked so hard to earn money to buy had been stolen along with anything else the thieves could carry away.

George Caldwell went to the police station to report the theft but was told that it was a low priority. His car was one of twenty-nine that had been broken into the previous night. The World's Fair attracted a lot of tourists who were prime targets for criminals. Chuck was heartbroken, but the spectacle and wonder of visiting a World's Fair helped ease his pain.

The World's Fair was spread out along three and a half miles of Lake Michigan shoreline. It covered 427 acres from Twelfth Street to Thirty-Ninth Street. Unlike the first World's Fair in Chicago that featured monochrome buildings that formed the "White City," this fair featured colorful buildings of a modern design.

As visitors toured various exhibit halls, they could see new concept automobiles and tour "homes of tomorrow" made of new building materials and techniques. Chuck remembered how wonderful it had been when his family had gotten a refrigerator in their Orrville home, but the future homes at the fair showed that dishwashers and air conditioning would also someday become commonplace.

While those exhibits successfully urged visitors to spend money to upgrade their homes and automobiles, other exhibits simply entertained. Big-game-hunter Frank Buck opened his Jungle Camp showing off the many trophy animals he had hunted. Children enjoyed an Enchanted Isle where they could run and play in a fairy tale setting. Robert Ripley displayed off the oddities that he wrote about in an Odditorium. The first Major League All-Star Baseball game was played during the fair's run at Comiskey Park.

The fair was not all fun, games and fantasy. Unfortunately, the realities of modern life and international politics intruded. The *Graf Zeppelin* appeared over the city on October 26, 1933. The sight of the massive airship from Nazi Germany angered some people. The 776-foot-long *Zeppelin* circled Lake Michigan for two hours like a floating billboard for National Socialism. It anchored at the Curtiss-Wright Airport, but remained there for less than half an hour before heading off to Akron, Ohio, ahead of bad weather.

Few people were sorry to see it go. The airship was a reminder of German Chancellor Adolf Hitler and his violent rise to power. If Chuck had seen it, he would have been fascinated and angered at the same time. Already a student of history, Chuck had been hearing stories about Hitler for a year. He may have been just a boy, but he knew a bully when he saw one.

Still, Chuck would have loved to have seen the huge airship floating over the city.

A few years later, his sister Barbara dated a young man who was the son of one of the engineers who designed the 784-foot-long *U.S.S. Macon*, a U.S. Navy airship that was supposed to serve as a flying aircraft carrier. Hangars in the airship carried five planes that could be launched and retrieved via a trapeze at the bottom of the airship. The *Macon* had a rigid hull filled with a dozen helium cells that provided the lift for the large airship. It had been christened on March 11, 1933, before the Chicago's World Fair opened and fairgoers would have appreciated seeing it more than the *Graf Zeppelin*. The *Macon* and its sister ship, the *Akron*, represented American ingenuity to many people, while the *Graf Zeppelin* represented totalitarianism.

Barbara Caldwell's high school picture. Courtesy of Chuck Caldwell.

With his sister's connection, Chuck was able to visit the airdock where the *Macon* had been built. When the hangar had been constructed in 1929 on the south side of Akron, it had been the largest building in the world without interior supports. It was 1,175 feet long, 325 feet wide, and 211 feet high.

Chuck was stunned by the size. "You could play ten football games in here at the same time," he told his father.

Actually, the hangar's 364,000 square feet of floor space could have accommodated only eight football fields. What also impressed Chuck was that the building seemed to have its own weather.

"You could see frost forming at the top even though it was warm on the ground," he said.

The *Akron* had crashed off the coast of New Jersey in April

1933 before the Caldwells had traveled to Chicago for the World's Fair. The accident killed seventy-three of the seventy-six people on board. The *Macon* would face a similar fate off the California coast in 1935, but luckily only two of the seventy-six people aboard were killed. German airships did not fare any better, the *Hindenburg* caught fire and burned, killing thirty-six of the ninety-seven people on board in 1937. Though not as deadly as either the *Akron* or *Macon* disasters, the fire was filmed and the casualties were civilians. These two factors combined to make the *Hindenburg* fire infamous and the ship that people remembered when airships were discussed.

The World's Fair exhibit that Chuck remembered best was the Sky Ride. Visitors rode elevators to the top of tall, steel towers that rose 628 feet into the air. One tower was on the mainland while the other tower stood 1,850 feet away across the lagoon on the fair's island, which had been built atop a reclaimed landfill. From the observation deck there, he could see far into the city and over Lake Michigan. On clear days, a person could also see into adjacent states.

An aerial track carried double-decker rocket cars across the lagoon and 210 feet above it for a distance of more than one-third of a mile to other tower. Chuck rode it from one side of the fair to the other and loved every foot of the trip.

Back home in Orrville, the Great Depression was taking hold. People were out of work and struggling to make ends meet. The collapse of the U.S. financial market was felt in small-town America as banks and businesses folded. Other businesses survived but with a severe reduction in trade because of rising unemployment.

George worked hard at his job. At one point, he taught a weekday Bible class for three years on top of his normal pastoral duties. He served on the faculty of the annual religious training schools held in Orrville, president of the Orrville Ministerial Association, member of the Chamber of Commerce, president and secretary of the Rotary Club at various times, and an organizer of the Orrville High School Booster Club. He did all of this work and earned roughly $1,100 a year.

George and Ellen knew how to stretch out that money, though.

The Caldwell home was one of only three houses on their block and behind the house was a nice big backyard. Ellen planted a beautiful flower garden immediately behind the house with a walking path that wound around, a bird bath, even a fish pond with floating glass balls in it. It was Ellen's oasis of serenity where she could enjoy the scent and color of the flowers and appreciate God's artistry.

The garden ended at a trellis with lots of hanging flowers and plants. Right behind that trellis and hidden from view from the house, George and Chuck planted a vegetable garden. They grew corn, potatoes, carrots, even strawberries. Of course, Chuck made sure to steer his father away from things like asparagus and Brussel sprouts. Although Chuck loved strawberries, they were a lot of work as he spent hours picking invading insects off of the berries.

Ellen canned all of the vegetables that came out of the garden in glass jars and stored them in a section of the basement she had set aside for her food storage. She also canned meats like roast beef whenever she could afford to buy some.

One of Chuck's favorite meals was his mother's roast beef. "She would put it in a bowl with some gravy and sometimes a potato but not always. It was delicious. She was a good cook," Chuck said with an expression on his face that said he could remember the taste of delicious meal.

After dinner, it was Chuck and Barbara's responsibility to wash the dishes.

"I'll do the washing and you do the drying," Barbara always offered.

Chuck would agree, but then he would be surprised at how much longer he wound up stuck in the kitchen while Barbara was off reading a magazine or listening to the radio. Chuck thought he was clever when he started offering to wash and she dried.

"I'll be darned if she still wasn't done before I was. I don't know how she did it," Chuck said.

The railroads that ran through Orrville were the life blood of the town, carrying goods from various industries in town, creating jobs, and connecting Orrville to the world. As the Depression wore on, men would sometimes hop into open railcars to travel from town to town in search of work or just a handout. Most of them were just out of work and struggling to get by. Occasionally, one of these hobos would knock at the rear door of the Caldwell home and ask for something to eat. Ellen would always ask him if he was willing to work. If the hobo said "no," she sent him on his way. If he said "yes," sometimes she would have an odd job for him to do like raking leaves, but more often than not, she would simply make him a sandwich.

Once Chuck was old enough, he decided to get himself a paper route to earn his own money. He couldn't rely on his parents for candy, baseball cards, comics, and even inexpensive clay. He actually wound up with three different paper routes because not all of the local papers were dailies. Orrville lay between Wooster and Canton so Chuck found himself delivering the Orrville *Courier Crescent* on Mondays and Thursdays, the *Canton Repository* on Tuesdays and Thursdays, and the Wooster *Daily Record* every day except Sunday. They were all afternoon papers, which worked out fine. He'd fold the newspapers after school and set out on the day's route. What wasn't so fine was that all of the routes were in different areas of Orrville. He had a paper route in every area of town except where he lived. Chuck found himself having to walk all over town because he didn't have a bicycle. It made the time it took him to complete the route three times longer. The summers were the worst. By the time he finished his route, he was dripping in sweat.

Delivering newspapers was hard work for a pre-teen. Not only did he have to walk everywhere lugging a heavy bag of newspapers across his shoulders, but he had to deal with difficult customers.

One snowy winter a woman on his route called him. "I didn't get my paper," she told Chuck, who had just finished up his route and was getting warm near a radiator in his house.

He knew very well that he had folded the newspaper into his familiar triangle shape and sent it sailing like a boomerang onto the woman's circular porch.

"I'm sure I delivered one," Chuck told the woman. "Did you look around the other side of the porch?"

"No, but it's not on the porch," the woman insisted.

Chuck suppressed a groan because he knew, *he just knew*, where he would find that newspaper.

So he reluctantly promised to bring the woman another newspaper. He wanted to keep his customers satisfied. He bundled up in a heavy coat, hat, and mittens, and trudged through the falling snow across town with a single newspaper and what should he see when he arrived at the woman's house? The newspaper he had delivered lay on the other side of the porch.

To add insult to injury, since the Great Depression was still going on, many of his customers would delay their payments or not pay him at all. Some weeks he didn't make anything for all of the hard work he put in.

"There was one lady on my route who still owes me money," he said.

When Chuck did get paid, though, he put away money into a savings account at the Orrville National Bank. His goal was to save sixteen dollars so that he could buy himself a bicycle that would make traveling his three paper routes all over Orrville much easier. It took him months to save that amount, but he finally saw the end in sight when he could withdraw his money and buy the bike he had chosen.

Chuck walked into the two-story bank building with its large sandstone pillars facing West Market Street. He clutched his latest deposit in his hand. Bank Manager Ed Seas, who was a member of Chuck's father's congregation, saw Chuck and waved to him.

"Two more payments and it's mine," Chuck told Seas as he held up the money for his latest deposit.

Seas shook his head. "No, I think you've got enough. It's already yours."

Chuck wasn't the best math student, but he kept careful track of his money. "No, I've got two more payments."

Seas smiled. "No, it's already paid for."

Chuck walked up to the teller window and asked the teller to check the balance on his account. The week before he knew that he had been a couple dollars short of the magic sixteen-dollar amount, but the teller told him that he had sixteen dollars in his account.

Chuck never knew for sure, and Seas never told him, but Chuck always believed that the bank manager had made up the difference for him.

Whatever the truth was, it enabled Chuck to buy his new bike and speed up his newspaper deliveries.

As Chuck prepared to enter Orrville High School, his sister graduated as her class salutatorian and began taking classes at Wooster College. Although the college was only fourteen miles away from Orrville, Barbara decided that she wanted to live at college. After all, she wanted to participate in a lot of the clubs and sing in the choir so she would be spending long days at school and didn't need to be driving back and forth a lot.

She also left big expectations among the Orrville High School faculty that Chuck couldn't live up to. He was never as strong a student as his sister. In fact, one of his teachers, who had also taught Barbara, told Chuck after he had been in her class awhile, "I can't believe you're Barbara's brother."

Orrville High had around 300 students enrolled, and Chuck's class was made up of seventy-six boys and girls. The school itself was relatively small. Original plans had called for a school to have a swimming pool, but funds had run out and so the pool was scrapped in favor of a small gymnasium.

With some extra room in their house once Barbara moved away, the Caldwells decided to take in boarders to make some additional money. George was doing well as the pastor at the Presbyterian Church. Attendance at his services had grown so much that by 1937, the membership needed to build an addition onto the rear of the building. Being a pastor had never been a high-paying profession and the Caldwells now had a daughter in college.

Chuck moved his room up into the attic and his old bedroom and his sister's old room were rented out. Soon, Ronald Sayer, a high school chemistry professor, and Alexander Hamilton, a chemist at Century Wood Preserving in Orrville, were joining the Caldwells for evening meals.

When Chuck and his father returned home from the Gettysburg reunion in 1938, Chuck began to embellish his scrapbook full of signatures and photos. He drew little Confederate and Union flags, depending on which side the soldier fought. He cut small pictures from a map with little depictions of various Civil War battlefields on it. He was always seeing ways to make something a little bit more creative and artistic.

It was just the latest form of artistic expression for Chuck. He had truly taken to drawing and sculpting. In February of

1938, he crafted busts of George Washington and Abraham Lincoln that were displayed in the window of the Orrville National Bank to celebrate the birthdays of both presidents that month.

Encouraged by the response to that display, Chuck decided that he was ready to start showing more of his work. He entered a model of a Confederate camp he created that featured dozens of inch-high soldiers in the Wayne County Hobby Exposition sponsored by the Wooster 20-30 Club, a chapter of the national service organization. The show was held in the Wooster High School cafeteria in April and it drew more than 100 entries from displays of China elephants to a working model of an oil derrick. The exhibitors, most of them adults, came from all around Wayne County.

Chuck set up his display with care, arranging the figures in precise locations on the set that he had created. Then he stood behind the display and watched as people passed by to stare at his art work. By the end of the evening, he waited anxiously for the results.

The exhibits were judged in seven classes: photography, handicraft, natural history, creative art, mechanical and technical displays, models, and collections. Three prizes were awarded in each category and two grand prize cups were also awarded.

The grand prize winners that year were Mrs. Russell Lehman and Carl Gurr of Wooster – Lehman had a handkerchief collection, and Gurr displayed a mahogany chair with an upholstered seat, patterned after the style of Spanish Court furniture of the eighteenth century. Chuck didn't even win in his category.

He was disappointed, but it was about what he had expected. He was a self-taught artist because art—his best subject—wasn't a subject taught in his high school. He would imagine something that he wanted to draw or shape from clay and just create it. He hadn't been sure whether he could make something worthy of prize.

Chuck continued working at his art because he loved it. He also loved *Gone With the Wind* when it premiered in movie theaters in 1939. Some people might tell you the movie was a love story between Scarlett O'Hara and Rhett Butler, but for Chuck, it was a movie about the Civil War and the defeat of the South. He marveled not so much at the acting, but at the scenes that showed large vistas that helped him imagine the country during the Civil War.

One of the *Gone With the Wind* dioramas that Chuck created while in high school. Courtesy of Chuck Caldwell.

The scene in the movie that showed the rail yard after the burning of Atlanta when Scarlett sees all of the Confederate casualties laying on the ground stuck in his head. Chuck began sketching and creating two-inch-high figures to populate the setting he had painted.

When he finished it, Freedlander's Department Store in Wooster asked him to display the model in their window. *Gone With the Wind* was playing in town and the store owner thought the display would help attract customers to come in and buy whatever they might need.

Chuck Caldwell's award-winning *Gone With the Wind* Diorama. Courtesy of Chuck Caldwell.

Chuck didn't have long to enjoy his mild fame. News reached the family in early April 1940 that George's father had died from throat cancer. It had only been diagnosed the previous fall and had spread rapidly. Charles Caldwell had been preaching at Penney Farms since he had returned there with his new bride in 1932.

George Caldwell had his father's body brought to Orrville and Charles was buried in Crown Hill Cemetery alongside his first wife.

When May rolled around, Chuck entered his *Gone With the Wind* display in the 1940 Wayne County Hobby Exposition. His final display featured about 400 different clay figures in addition to the ones he had drawn into the background scenery. The movie had set a record for Academy Award nominations (thirteen) and wins (eight) at the end of February, so people were interested in seeing Chuck's diorama.

More than 2,000 people visited the seventy-five exhibits in the Wooster Armory during the exhibition. This time, Chuck took first place in the Youth Division.

Besides showing off his artistic talent, Chuck also worked on his musical skills. He started playing the snare drum in high school. He played as part of the school's sixty-six-piece marching band. One of his friends, Dick Fugittt, also played drums, and he was so good at it that he eventually started his own band.

As Chuck finished up his junior year in high school, Barbara graduated from Wooster College with a degree in political science.

Barbara had always been a good student. The same couldn't be said for Chuck. He struggled with his classes and would have preferred drawing scenes from a book rather than reading it.

Barbara did take some time out of her schedule to drive Chuck to Wooster to take his driver's test. During his test, a highway patrolman rode along with him asking him to make turns, stop for lights, and display his knowledge of traffic laws.

Chuck thought that he was doing well. Then the highway patrolman had him pull over to the curb behind another car.

As soon as Chuck pulled to a stop, another car pulled up right behind him close to his rear bumper.

The highway patrolman next to Chuck turned to him and said, “You can pull out now.”

But Chuck couldn’t. He had pulled up too close to the car in front of him and didn’t have enough room between the three cars to squeeze out.

He failed his test.

When he returned the next month to re-take the driving test, he made sure to leave plenty of room in front of him when he pulled over, and he passed the test.

Now that Chuck was mobile, he and his friends were able to take girls on dates that weren’t within walking distance of the girl’s home. They would search the newspapers to find out where the popular bands were playing. He saw Horace Hyte in Akron and Tommy Dorsey at Chippewa Lake, among others.

“We would get four in a car for a double date and drive to Myers Lake or Summit Beach where they had beautiful dance halls,” Chuck said. “I wasn’t a good dancer, but I liked to dance. We’d have a great time for a couple bucks.”

On one occasion, Chuck took a date to see the Glenn Miller Band playing at the Palace Theater in Cleveland. He had a good seat about five rows from the front. The problem was that a man in a “sporty coat” kept pushing his right arm against Chuck’s left arm for control of the arm rest between the two seats.

Eventually, the man got up and walked away. Chuck thought he’d been victorious in the battle of the arm rest.

“Then I realized the guy was walking towards the stage and Glenn Miller was announcing that an old friend was playing out at the Spanish Tavern and had come to sit in on the drums. ‘Here’s Gene Krupa,’” Chuck explained.

To have even a couple dollars on hand for weekly dates required something more than a newspaper route or even three. For the summer of 1940, Chuck took a job at the Century Wood Preserving plant in Orrville. The plant made railroad ties and also the treated timber used for building wooden bridges. The wood was treated with creosote, an oily and smelly compound that prevents moisture damage and repels insects. Former employee Roger Scott said, "If you lived on the east side of downtown Orrville, the creosote odor was always thick in the air. It would cling to your clothes and hair."

Joe Lay, the plant manager, tried to give the work to high school boys who were preparing for college and needed to save money.

Wooden ties were piled on railroad dollies and taken into high-pressure rooms that forced creosote into the wood. The ties were then taken outside to the yard where steam cranes stacked them into towers up to twenty-five high. The yards stretched more than mile along Orr Street from east of Orrville Cemetery to east of Church Street. Though not nearly as wide as it was long, it was blocks wide.

Chuck worked mainly in the yard among the tall towers of wooden ties. His main job was to drive S irons into the ends of the treated ties to keep them from splitting. It was the kind of work that required more youth and energy than experience. For the higher-up ties, Chuck would stand on a scaffold hanging on the side of the tie pile. He carried a two-pound sledge and canvas sack full of S irons. He would line up the S-shaped pieces of iron on the end of the tie and then hit it left, right, and center. Three hits for a half a penny. He could drive 1,000 S irons in a day and earn five dollars.

After his first day of work, Chuck's arms and shoulders were swollen and sore, but he kept at it and the pain eventually disappeared as he added muscle to his skinny frame. Those were the weeks he considered himself lucky.

His work alternated between working a week in the yard with working in the treatment room where the water was removed from the wood and it was treated with creosote.

After Chuck's first couple days working in the treatment room, his mother fixed up a shower in the basement of the house because even after driving home in an open car, Chuck reeked of creosote. He wasn't allowed to walk through the house after coming home from work. He came in the side door by the kitchen and went downstairs to try and wash the creosote and its smell from his body. His clothes picked up so much of it that he could stand his pants up in the shower room.

"My mother would put tea compresses on my eyes because they were fogged up with creosote," Chuck said.

He considered himself lucky. The men whose job it was to carry the ties from finishing to treating and then out to the yard were big men with one shoulder larger than the other from always carrying the ties on the same shoulder.

Many of those large men were from Mississippi and apparently prone to violence. Chuck once saw a man killed in the plant lunch room.

"These guys were playing cards in the lunch room," he said. "I don't know what was said. I wasn't that close to it. I heard an argument and I saw them carry this body and his head out into a truck."

An argument over the card game had gone too far and one man had pulled a knife on the other man and used it. They weren't the only employees killed while Chuck worked there, but the other deaths were job related.

Chuck just shrugged off the incident and did his job.

As he entered his senior year in Orrville High School, Chuck started looking to improve his resume. After all, he was not a star student or athlete. He gave up the band to work as the business manager for *The Red Rider*, Orrville High's newspaper. He was also part of the technical staff for the National Thespian Society, which meant Chuck painted scenery for the organization's various productions like "Going Places" by Glenn Hughes. It was the senior play performed by the Class of 1941.

Chuck, his father George, and his grandfather Charles. Courtesy of Chuck Caldwell.

His friends started applying to different colleges. Chuck applied to only one. It was the one where he had always wanted to attend. The University of Alabama was Chuck's dream school and he got in. The *Courier Crescent* even ran a small article about Chuck's acceptance at the school with the headline, "Charles Caldwell Finds His Dream Is True".

The university in Tuscaloosa had nearly 5,000 students

along with a commerce school and a medical school and many other courses of study that Chuck preferred. It even had art classes that he could take. His main interest in the school, though, was its football team. He had been interested in the Crimson Tide since 1935 and had even started making clay models of the players.

Now he would be attending the same school as some of his favorite sports heroes and studying art and history. Things don't always work out the way a person plans, though.

1941
BECOMING A MARINE

Chuck Caldwell never met William G. Little, but if such a meeting had ever happened, it would have been a certainty that Chuck would have nearly shaken the man's hand off of his arm while thanking him profusely.

As a young man, Little had wanted to attend an Ivy League university, but after his brother died, he decided that it would be better for him to stay closer to his home and family in Livingston, Alabama. He enrolled at the University of Alabama "in the fall of 1892 with a pair of cleats, a leather football, and tales of the new sport that had captured the imagination of the Northeast and Middlewest," Winston Groom wrote in *The Crimson Tide*.

Though a version of football had been played for decades, it had only come to resemble modern football in the years leading up to Little enrolling in the University of Alabama. This is the game that Little had learned while attending the Phillips-Exeter Academy in Andover, Massachusetts. He loved playing and put together a team of nineteen fellow University of Alabama classmates. He taught them the game and they began practicing. The University of Alabama football team played its first football game on November 11, 1892, and won 56-0. It didn't matter that the opposing team had been made up of Birmingham High School seniors. Alabama's drive to win had started.

By the time, Chuck enrolled in the university in 1941, the Crimson Tide had won four national championships in 1925, 1926, 1930, and 1934. It had also won Chuck's undying loyalty.

Though Chuck was an artist, he had not considered enrolling in art school. He had not considered attending any other college. For him, it was the University of Alabama or nothing. It was a childhood wish that he made come true.

Chuck's last day working at the Century Wood Preserving Plant was on August 29, 1941. At the end of the day, he collected his final week's pay of $26.50. Then he drove home to his basement shower and spent half an hour scrubbing himself free of creosote and its stench for the last time.

The next three days were a blur as he packed to leave for the University of Alabama. He had to decide what a college student needed and leave the rest behind. He stuffed his clothes and art supplies into a suitcase and boxes.

Finally on September 2, the Caldwells climbed into their car and headed south from Orrville. Though Tuscaloosa, Alabama, is only 750 miles southwest of Orrville, the Caldwells turned the trip into a mini-vacation that took four days. They stopped to visit with family in southern Ohio. They made another stop in Nashville, Tennessee, to sightsee and tour Vanderbilt University and the Hermitage, President Andrew Jackson's home. Chuck, ever the history buff, enjoyed the latter stop.

Pulling onto the campus of the University of Alabama on September 6 took Chuck's breath away.

"I felt like a kid who had gotten into Heaven," Chuck said.

He had seen pictures of the campus, but he had never been here before. Photos couldn't capture the size of the university or the number of people he saw walking around the grounds. The university had more students, not including employees, than Orrville had residents. It looked like Gettysburg had looked during the seventy-fifth anniversary in 1938 or Chicago during the World's Fair. The university packed all of those students into an area much smaller than Orrville. Gone were the cottage-style homes and the downtown two-story businesses. In their place were buildings like Woods Hall, the four-story brick building that ran along the northern side of the quad and was the first building constructed as the campus began rebuilding itself from its burning by Union forces during the Civil War. Then there was Clark Hall, which resembled a European cathedral with windows that were three-stories tall and Tutwiler Hall, focus of the women's campus, with its half dozen grand columns at the entryway.

This was a place where Chuck had sought to be for most of his young life. His awe of the university grandeur did not even dim when he discovered that the huge, monument-like buildings did not contain equally cavernous interior rooms. Clayton Hall, one of the freshman dormitories, wasn't anything fancy. Chuck's small dorm room was barely larger than his bedroom at home and he had to share his room with a good ol' boy from Alabama named Ralph Bugg. The three-story brick building was one of six matching men's dormitories that had been built two years previously.

Chuck didn't mind the dorm's plainness. It was still part of the University of Alabama. He had made it. Now he set his sights on his next goal.

Two days after arriving on campus, Chuck tried out to be manager of the freshman football team and got the job. He was now part of the Crimson Tide.

The University of Alabama had used the nickname since 1907 when, during a game against Auburn in Birmingham, Alabama's team had churned the playing field into a sea of red mud. A sportswriter had first used the term to describe Alabama's surging offense on the field during the game.

Chuck could have tried out to be a player on the freshman team, but he was no fool. He was about two-thirds the size of the average freshman football player. He knew there was no way he had the size or skill to play football for Alabama. Besides, even if by some miracle he had made the team, he might not have lived to enjoy it.

"The freshmen teams were the blocking dummies for the varsity," Chuck said. "It toughened them up for the next year."

As manager, Chuck showed up at practices earlier than the rest of the team in order to have all of the equipment ready to use when practice actually started. He carried spare shoelaces and bandages in his pocket in case the players needed them. During practice, he ran errands and cleaned up after the players.

"I got picked on by the players because I was small. It was all right, though, because I was part of the team. I was part of the Great Crimson Tide," Chuck said with pride evident in his voice.

Chuck may have been small, but the varsity football players were not that huge either, at least compared to today's standards. Chuck stood five feet six inches tall and weighed 120 pounds. In 1940, the average offensive lineman was six-feet one-inch tall and weighed 221 pounds.

After practices, Chuck stayed later than anyone else to clean up after the team. He got to travel with the team when they played away games, including playing Tulane University at Tulane Stadium in New Orleans where the Sugar Bowl was played from 1934 to 1974. Part of his job at away games was identifying University of Alabama players for radio announcers. He kept a box containing cards with each player's name, number, and stats on it. As substitutions were made, he would switch cards so that the stack of cards in front of the announcer represented the team on the field.

A week after Chuck started as team manager, he received his class schedule for the fall semester. He was taking biology, history, Spanish, English, and art. The only class that interested him was the art class, his first ever. He could have cared less about the others. They neither helped him with his art or with football. They were classes he needed to graduate, though.

He also joined the school's Army ROTC program. It was a required course for all freshman if they were physically able.

The University of Alabama had fourteen commissioned U. S. Army officers assigned to the university's program to help train future military officers. Chuck certainly didn't want to join the Army. Chuck's memories of ROTC were marching around a lot and practicing with an old Springfield rifle.

Mixed in with classes, football, and ROTC, Chuck pledged Delta Chi, a fraternity that had been on campus since 1927.

Chuck's freshman photo at the University of Alabama. Courtesy of Chuck Caldwell.

Chuck worked hard and long hours in college. Unfortunately, not enough of that work went toward his classwork and studying. Most of his time was spent with the football team. Allowances were made and tutors provided to help the athletes keep their grades up, but that perk didn't extend to the team managers. Chuck was on his own there, and he had never been a strong student to start.

His grades began looking so bad that he was thinking that he might have to drop out of college. The end of the semester was approaching in the middle of December 1941. He knew that he wasn't prepared for his final exams and he needed to be. This would be his last chance to pull his grades out of the dumpster, but he didn't have any time to study. He staggered back to his dorm room late in the evening after a game or practice, and then he'd get up early to eat breakfast and go to his morning classes. In the afternoons, he had ROTC or football practice, which ate up any free time he had.

For strong students, class time could provide enough instruction for at least a passing grade. Because Chuck was only an average student at best, he needed to study outside of the classroom in order to maintain his grades at a decent level. What worried him the most was that he knew how hard he and his parents had scraped and saved to come up with the $300 a quarter tuition needed, not to mention his living expenses. If Chuck had to drop out, it would all be wasted.

As Chuck grew more and more skeptical about his chances of passing his classes that semester, he decided that he needed a Plan B in case he wouldn't be returning to the university after the Christmas break.

On December 1, he rode a bus into Tuscaloosa and talked to a Marine recruiter about enlisting. He had some military training from his time in the ROTC, but he also knew that he didn't want to join the Army. Chuck signed all of the paperwork needed to enlist in the U.S. Marine Corps. All that was left for him to do was to take and pass his final physical. Even this was a test he wasn't completely sure that he could pass. He arranged it so that he wouldn't be inducted until after Christmas.

Now he just had to wait and see how he did on his final exams.

On Sunday, December 7, Chuck was getting some rare study time in when his buddies rushed into the room.

"The Japs just bombed Pearl Harbor!" Ralph Bugg yelled.

Chuck was stunned. He knew from his roommate's tone that something was wrong, but he wasn't quite sure what. He knew the Japanese had been fighting China and talking aggressively toward the United States.

"Where's Pearl Harbor?" Chuck asked.

His roommate shrugged. "I don't know."

They had to dig out an atlas to locate Pearl Harbor and discover that it was in Hawaii, which wasn't even a U.S. state at the time, but it was a U.S. territory.

Chuck and his friends, along with millions of Americans, spent the day huddled around the radio listening for the latest information. When the afternoon newspapers came out, they rushed to buy them. All thought of Christmas was forgotten as Americans sought information regarding what had happened at Pearl Harbor, Hawaii.

The Imperial Japanese Navy had launched a surprise attack against the U.S. Navy base at Pearl Harbor at 7:48 a.m., which would have been 12:48 p.m. in Alabama. During the attack, 353 Japanese aircraft flew from six aircraft carriers in two waves to bomb the base. Eight U.S. battleships docked there were damaged and half of them sunk. Three cruisers, three destroyers, a training ship, and a minelayer were also damaged or sunk. The Japanese destroyed 188 U.S. aircraft. The human casualties were even worse with 2,403 people killed and 1,178 wounded.

The cost to the Japanese for the attack had been light with twenty-nine aircraft and five midget submarines destroyed and sixty-five airmen and sailors killed or wounded. It had been a great victory for the Japanese, even if it had been a sneak attack against an enemy that didn't even know it was at war with Japan.

Chuck hadn't been born when World War I had been fought so the scope of this destruction was unimaginable, particularly since it had just happened. The casualties were still being counted. This wasn't history. It wasn't a Civil War battle that he was reading about. It was the present. It was reality.

He listened the next day as President Franklin D. Roosevelt gave his famous speech to Congress and a still-stunned country, declaring "December 7, 1941 - a date which will live in infamy - the United States of America was suddenly and deliberately attacked by naval and air forces of the Empire of Japan."

Chuck and the United States learned just how aggressive Japan had become. The president said, "The attack yesterday on the Hawaiian islands has caused severe damage to American naval and military forces. Very many American lives have been lost. In addition, American ships have been reported torpedoed on the high seas between San Francisco and Honolulu.

"Yesterday, the Japanese government also launched an attack against Malaya.

"Last night, Japanese forces attacked Hong Kong.

"Last night, Japanese forces attacked Guam.

"Last night, Japanese forces attacked the Philippine Islands.

"Last night, the Japanese attacked Wake Island.

"This morning, the Japanese attacked Midway Island."

He then went on to declare war against Japan, saying, "Hostilities exist. There is no blinking at the fact that our people, our territory and our interests are in grave danger.

"With confidence in our armed forces – with the unbounding determination of our people – we will gain the inevitable triumph – so help us God.

"I ask that the Congress declare that since the unprovoked and dastardly attack by Japan on Sunday, Dec. 7, a state of war has existed between the United States and the Japanese Empire."

As the realization settled on Chuck that the Japanese had attacked the United States and that the two countries were now at war, Chuck's first thought was that he now had an excuse to do poorly on his exams. Then as he realized what he was thinking, he felt shame. People had died. They had been bombed, shot, and burned to death, and here he sat worried about his grades.

Chuck left school on December 15 without even taking his finals. It didn't matter now. Men his age were joining the military in droves, and he was one of them. With the need for recruits suddenly greater, the U.S. Marine Corps lowered the enlistment age from eighteen years old to seventeen and then reduced the length of boot camp from eight weeks to four weeks. It would eventually be expanded so that by the time the war ended, recruits received sixteen weeks of training. Enlistment periods were extended from three years to the length of the war. Within two months of the attack on Pearl Harbor, the number of Marine recruits grew from 2,869 men in four battalions to over 15,000 men in thirteen battalions.

Chuck headed home on the train to tell his parents the news that he was going to be a Marine. He had made his decision before the United States went to war, but Pearl Harbor hadn't caused him to doubt his decision. It had only strengthened his resolve. His parents were worried for him and proud of him at the same time. Christmas was a somewhat subdued holiday that year. Not only was the country and world at war, but Chuck was going to be one of the tens of thousands of young men sent overseas to possibly die fighting against the very soldiers who had started a war against the United States.

Chuck Caldwell's United States Marine Corps identification. Courtesy of Chuck Caldwell.

A few days after Christmas on December 30, Chuck hugged his parents and kissed them goodbye. His mother held back her tears, but she hugged him almost to the point of clinging. Chuck climbed into his sister's car and Barbara drove him to Cleveland, an hour and fifteen minutes away. Barbara planned to spend the night with a friend in town just in case Chuck failed his final physical and needed a ride home. It was a possibility, after all. Chuck was healthy, but he wasn't a large young man.

Barbara dropped her brother off at the municipal building in Cleveland. She didn't come inside with him because what aspiring Marine wants to be seen with his sister, especially for a physical exam? They said their goodbyes at the curb and Chuck headed inside.

The building's auditorium was filled with hundreds of young men sitting at tables talking with recruiters, getting physical examinations, or simply sitting and waiting to be directed somewhere. Chuck checked in and sat down to wait for his turn with a doctor.

The exam was quick and basic. Chuck walked from station to station in his boxers, holding his folder of paperwork in front of him like Adam's fig leaf. The upshot of it was that Chuck made it into the United States Marine Corps with a half an inch and a pound to spare. The minimum requirement for Marines at the time was that they weigh at least 120 pounds and stand at least five feet six inches tall. Chuck's picture on his Marine identification shows a young man standing nearly five foot eight inches tall. That is, until the doctor pushed down on his puffy hair.

Once he passed his physical, Chuck got dressed and took a seat in a different area of the auditorium. From here, small groups of recruits were taken into a room where they were sworn into the Corps. The serial numbers were assigned sequentially so Chuck knew that he had become the $342{,}764^{th}$ U. S. Marine to serve the United States.

The Crescent-Courier noted that Chuck had been the first

local man to enlist in the Marines.

The group of recruits that Chuck was sworn in with consisted of eight men, most of whom were from Ohio, but a couple were from Pennsylvania and one was from Kentucky. Another recruit was a young man from Allentown, Pennsylvania, named Paul Heller. He was much taller than Chuck, but Heller had lied about his age and was only fifteen. This group of recruits would stay together all through boot camp, only separating as they were sent to different units to serve.

"They asked us when we wanted to leave," Chuck recalled. "We talked it over and figured why wait. We said, 'Tonight.'"

The recruits were taken to the train station next door at the municipal building and loaded onto a train filled with other recruits. Chuck was in a Pullman car filled with twenty-seven other enlistees. A sergeant handed each recruit a memorandum that outlined how recruits were expected to behave on the trip south. Apparently, the memorandum was needed because, "Complaints have been received by this office that men have been parading up and down the aisles of the trains in a most indecent manner, especially upon retireing (sic), and going to the toilet. You are instructed to refrain from exposing yourself, as there may be ladies in the car." The memorandum reminded the new recruits that they now represented the U.S. Marines and were expected to conduct themselves accordingly.

The train pulled out of Cleveland at 12:30 a.m. headed for South Carolina. It was filled with Marines, or rather, Marine recruits called "boots." Unlike the other armed forces that consider an enlistee a soldier or sailor as soon as they swear the oath, Marine recruits have to earn the right to be called a Marine. Until that time, they are treated like dirt.

Chuck didn't know it, but he was enjoying his last, few peaceful hours for a long time.

Frank Sloza was a bit older than the typical recruit. In his twenties, Frank had had a career before he enlisted. He had been a boxer from Masury, Ohio, who sometimes worked as a sparring partner with other professional boxers. As he and Chuck talked during the long train ride, Chuck took a liking to him.

The seats of the train were designed to convert to bunks so that travelers could sleep on overnight trips. Chuck had the upper bunk above Frank. Frank was an avid motorcyclist and his boots were the smelliest things that Chuck had ever caught a whiff of. They smelled worse than creosote if that was possible. Between the movement of the train and the smell of Frank's boots, Chuck felt like he slept that night on a garbage scow.

Chuck sent his parents a postcard at each stop that the train made. The recruits ate heartily at each meal. For breakfast on New Year's Day, Chuck ate oatmeal, tomato juice, milk, scrambled eggs, bacon, and rolls. He told his parents that the food was good, but "no comparison with Mother's cooking as if anything could be!!"

As the train wound through Kentucky and Tennessee and into South Carolina, 1941 became 1942. Chuck's beloved Crimson Tide was in Texas to play the Southwest Conference Champions Texas A&M in the Cotton Bowl on New Year's Day. Had he managed to pass his final college exams, Chuck would have been with them. Alabama would go on to win that game 29-21 by intercepting seven A&M passes and recovering five fumbles. For all his enthusiastic support of the Crimson Tide, Chuck wouldn't learn of the outcome of the game for quite some time.

Yemassee, South Carolina, took its name from a Native American tribe in the area. It became important to Marine boots because of the train depot, which was the junction point on the main line with the Charleston and West Carolina Railroad. It had brought in thousands of young men over the years on their way to Parris Island and carried them home afterward.

When Chuck's train stopped at Yemassee, a Marine sergeant greeted the recruits by telling them to haul their asses off the train or they would regret it. Chuck and the other young men hurried off the train and were crammed into the rear of trucks for a forty-mile ride to Parris Island. It would be a busy month at Yemassee and Parris Island. During January alone, 9,206 recruits would arrive for training.

New recruits await trucks to take them from Yemassee, S. C., to Parris Island. Courtesy of onlyinyourstate.com.

Parris Island had originally been used as a naval base in the 1890s before politics caused the base to be moved to Charleston, South Carolina, in 1909. It also served short stints as an officer's training school and military prison before finding its true calling as a Marine recruit training base in 1915.

Before 1929, everyone coming to the island arrived on a ferry from the Port Royal docks. A causeway and two-gauge steel bridge were completed that year that allowed motorized vehicles onto the island and made it easier to get people onto and off the island.

Chuck came to call Parris Island "the land that time forgot," but that was more because of what would happen to him there rather than how it looked.

Still, the base did look somewhat like a remote village decades behind the mainland. While there were some brick buildings used for base operations, the majority of structures were Quonset huts. These buildings resembled very large half-barrels with doors on either end. They looked temporary and there were so many on the island to house the massive inflow of recruits that the base had a temporary look.

The sergeant started yelling at the boots to get out of the truck and to fall in as soon as the truck stopped in front of the brick mess hall on base.

"I was called things I'd never even heard before," Chuck said, shaking his head. "I don't know where they got those words."

The recruits were ordered into the mess hall where they gave up their clothes and received their allotment of two sets of pajamas, two sheets, a pillow case, two blankets, a pair of dungarees, an overcoat, a bar of soap, and a towel. Then they were fitted for their uniforms.

"With each divestment, a trait is lost; the discard of a garment marks the quiet death of idiosyncrasy. I take off my socks; gone is a propensity for stripes, of checks, or even solids; ended is a tendency to combine purple socks with brown tie. My socks henceforth will be tan. They will neither be soiled, nor rolled, nor gaudy, nor restrained, nor holey. They will be tan. The only other thing they may be is clean," Robert Leckie wrote *in My Helmet for My Pillow.*

Because Chuck was on the smaller end of the size range for a Marine, the only boots that were available that would fit him and some of the other smaller recruits were hobnail boots left over from World War I.

"When we walked on the macadam, we shot sparks out," Chuck said.

Following the clothes, the next thing the recruits lost was their hair. It fell to a few quick swipes of the barber's blades.

They were then shown to Quonset huts that could sleep sixteen men in a room. Gone with their clothes was their privacy as well. If a drill instructor chose to, he could open a recruit's mail and read it to the platoon.

Chuck and the others were assigned to the First Marine Recruit Battalion and separated into six platoons of sixty-four men each. They would spend two weeks learning to march and drill, then two weeks on the rifle range, and a week of bayonet training. Chuck wondered if training was so short because the recruits would be cannon fodder. Prior to the war, Marines had trained for eight weeks.

"The only thing that had happened was Wake Island and we were hearing that we were going out to replace lost men," Chuck said.

The day after the attack on Pearl Harbor, the Japanese had attacked the military base on Wake Island, a two-and-a-half-square-mile coral atoll in the Pacific Ocean. The attack destroyed two-thirds of the Marine aircraft on the ground, but the defensive emplacements had still functioned. Following the initial attack, the Japanese attempted an amphibious assault on Dec. 11 to try and finish the job. The Marines beat them back and the Japanese suffered heavy losses.

The Navy tried to help the Marines, but their own forces were still suffering from the Pearl Harbor attack. The Marines held out against the overwhelming force of Japanese soldiers until Dec. 23.

Although the Japanese had eventually won the battle, it had cost them heavily. U.S. military and civilian deaths totaled 122 while the Japanese had lost more than 700 men. The Marines and Navy had also managed to sink two Japanese destroyers and shoot down twenty-four Japanese aircraft.

"We had no idea what the Japs were like," Chuck said. "To me, they were toymakers who didn't know how to make all the little tabs fit. We found out differently, though."

Chuck and the other boots quickly adjusted to a new routine at Parris Island that began at 4:30 a.m. and was filled with cleaning, close-order drills, lectures and other training. When the boots hit the rack at 9:30 p.m., most of them were asleep by the time "Taps" sounded at 10 p.m. However, the recruits often found themselves up past midnight as drill instructors tried to make up for the shorter overall time they had to train the recruits by making them work longer days. No matter how late they drilled, though, the boots were expected on the field with their gear by 6 a.m. the next morning.

Their days were structured following the orders of their drill instructors. Chuck's drill instructors were Corporal Lewindowski and Private First-Class Bolls. With the sudden jump in enlistees, sergeants were in short supply to act as drill instructors so some lower-ranked Marines were appointed as "Acting Jacks." Chuck never knew their first names. As far as he was concerned, their first names were both "Sir." Calling them anything else would have had him doing punishment work.

Drill instructors lived to make a recruit's life miserable. Their job was to break a slothful civilian down in order to build him back into a sharp and quick Marine as quickly as possible.

During his five weeks of training, Chuck marched miles and miles in full gear. If he wasn't marching, he was crawling on his stomach while other Marines fired dozens of live rounds over his head. He did all of this while under the verbal assault of drill instructors.

Chuck only truly got in trouble once. During drills, he was

moving his rifle from his right shoulder to his left when the bolt of the rifle grazed his helmet. It made a small noise, and Chuck thought the drill instructor was far enough away not to have heard it.

He was wrong.

The instructor stormed up to him and said, "Caldwell, you made a noise!"

Chuck explained that the bolt of his rifle had brushed the brim of his helmet. The instructor pushed his helmet down hard over his eyes so that Chuck couldn't see anything unless he looked down at the ground. He wasn't able to push the helmet up either. He had to drill for the rest of the day being unable to see in front of him.

After two weeks of drilling on base, Chuck's platoon marched with their packs on their backs in close order out to the rifle range, which was five miles away. When they arrived, they found their canvas seabags waiting for them. They bunked in six-man tents with no flooring.

The boots spent the next two weeks camping on the range and learning their rifles (God forbid, a boot made a mistake and called the rifle a gun!) with the goal of qualifying as a marksman. Boots needed to show that they were proficient shooting at targets 200, 300, 500, and 600 yards away. They also had to be able to shoot from standing, kneeling, sitting and prone positions, what the Marines referred to as "snapping in." To qualify with their weapons as a "guardsman", they had to score at least 275 out of 350 on the range. Sharpshooters scored at least 300 and rifle experts scored at least 315 points. It also meant a higher rate of pay. An expert marksman received five dollars a month more and a sharpshooter received three dollars a month more.

It was a lousy time to be on the range. Despite being in South Carolina, the January temperatures were cold as the wind blew in from the Atlantic Ocean. It also rained many days. The recruits still wore nothing other than their sweatshirts. Whether it was wet or dry, it was the only thing they had to wear. All of the shooting left Chuck's ears ringing for hours afterwards.

Their meals consisted of collard greens, barely cooked bacon, and black coffee three times a day.

"It was slop," Chuck said and certainly no match for the food that he had eaten on the train ride to Yemassee.

Very soon, many of the recruits were getting sick. At first, everyone thought it was the bad weather, but then they realized it was the food. A mess sergeant was caught cutting corners on the food. He was busted in rank to private and sent to the Navy prison in Portsmouth, New Hampshire. On the positive side, the food quickly got better.

With all the rain and wind on the range while Chuck's platoon was there, not a single person managed to qualify with their weapons. Even the boots who were familiar with weapons and had been hunting for years were unable to score 275. The recruits who were still on the island in May were given another chance to qualify, but by then, many of the others had already been shipped off to locations for advanced training.

Besides shooting on the range, the recruits were also shot while out there. The dispensary was located near the rifle range and the recruits were given the inoculations they would need for duty in the Pacific or Europe.

"Getting inoculations is inhuman. It is as though men were being fed into a machine 2 lines of corpsmen stand opposite and staggered, walk line, swab and stick," Leckie wrote.

Chuck's platoon marched back to the base after two weeks for their final week of training in bayonet and knife fighting and hand-to-hand combat. This wasn't taught by an instructor on base but a Philadelphia socialite named Anthony J. Drexel Biddle.

Biddle's opening demonstration of his qualifications impressed Chuck. He watched the sixty-six-year-old man step into the middle of a circle of a dozen men with bayoneted rifles. On Biddle's command, the men attacked one at a time. Unarmed, the old man swept in against the armed man and with a few moves relieved him of his weapon, plunging the bayonet into the sand. Then he would move onto the next Marine and the next, disarming each one of them and stabbing their bayonets into the ground.

Anthony J. Drexel Biddle gives Marines instruction on hand-to-hand combat at Parris Island. Courtesy of USmilitaryknives.com.

The demonstration was not always successful. Biddle was injured over the years. His worst injury put him in the hospital for two months.

Biddle may have circulated through the high society in Philadelphia, but he was a former Marine and expert in close-quarters combat. He had even written a book on the subject that was used by both Marines and the Federal Bureau of Investigation as a training guide.

Chuck didn't become as proficient as Biddle, particularly after only a week of training, but he learned enough to help him survive.

At the end of basic training, the boots had no graduation ceremony to mark their transition to becoming Marines. The new Marines were simply lined up and an officer walked down the line and told them whether they were staying at Parris Island for advanced training or moving on to another camp. Quantico, Virginia, taught radio school and aviation training. Sea school was at Norfolk, Virginia. Armorers school and clerical school were in Philadelphia, Pennsylvania.

Chuck stayed on the island and continued training. The original group of eight recruits whom he had been sworn in with and served through basic training with were divided up and sent to various duties. Chuck was assigned to an artillery battalion and began learning how to fire a 155-mm artillery gun. During the first week of July 1942, the battalion was loaded onto trucks and sent to Norfolk to board a converted steam liner and head for Australia.

"I wasn't scared," Chuck said. "I was going to take part in real history."

1942
ENTERING THE WAR

Word among the Marines on the dock at Norfolk was that the *Bloemfontein* was a Dutch cruise ship. They had visions of sailing into battle laying on deck chairs and sipping cocktails.

Then Chuck saw the ship with its peeling white paint exposing the gray steel beneath. What white paint did remain was gray from soot. Dents disrupted the smooth lines of the ship's hull. Chuck saw no color, decorations, and definitely no deck chairs; nothing that he associated with a luxury liner. He shook his head and decided that either somebody had been making a joke calling this derelict a luxury liner or that person had seen this ship in the dead of night with his eyes closed.

"The only thing this ship didn't have was holes in the side for the oarsmen's oars," Chuck said, comparing the ship to the ancient triremes that were powered by rows of galley slaves pulling on oars in unison.

But the *Bloemfontein* had been a Dutch cruise ship. Built in 1934, she had served as a passenger and cargo ship for the Holland Africa Line. She was 488 feet long and could travel up to sixteen knots. The ship could also carry more than 2,300 passengers and store 146,000 cubic feet of cargo.

During her early years, the *Bloemfontein* had made regular runs between Europe and Africa. An advertisement for the ship bragged that many of the first-class cabins had either a private bath or private shower. Children were supervised by a stewardess in the playful nursery. The ship also had an open-air swimming pool for first-class passengers and a canvas swimming pool for tourist-class passengers. Entertainment was extensive: "there are deck sports, dancing, bridge, film shows, children's parties, etc. regularly organized for those who wish to join," the ship's brochure proclaimed. Meals were served throughout the day. Breakfast alone included fruit, cereal, an egg dish, fresh-baked breads, preserves, and something to drink.

Ah! If only it had continued to be so.

The Dutch cruise ship turned troop transport *Bloemfontein*. Courtesy of Chuck Caldwell.

Once World War II started, the Holland to Africa route was disrupted and the *Bloemfontein* fell on hard times as it sat idle. Just as the war took boys of privilege and turned them into soldiers, it also took ships of luxury and turned them into troop transports. The *Bloemfontein*'s life as a luxury liner ended. When the U.S. Army leased the ship in 1941, it took on the personality of the servicemen it transported … rough and battered but pressing forward.

With her ability to haul a large number of men and a heavy weight of cargo, the *Bloemfontein* was a good choice to be used as a transport ship. Besides, Marines didn't need frills like private baths and semi-private rooms, and they certainly didn't need swimming pools and children's parties. Do away with the amenities and you had room for more troops.

The fresh Marines from Parris Island arrived by train at Norfolk on July 5, 1942. They had been trained, but not yet tested. However, they were no longer the green boots that had arrived in Parris Island at the beginning of the year. Chuck and the other Marines who had remained on Parris Island had even been able to go back to the rifle range and have a chance to certify as an expert marksman. Not that it did Chuck any good. He still couldn't certify.

The Marines spent their day on the docks of the Norfolk Naval Base loading the *Bloemfontein.* They carried boxes, bags, and barrels up the gangway and through an open hatch in the side of the ship that was much closer to the level of the docks.

Another sign that the ship was no luxury liner was that some of the men started sneezing as they walked aboard. The ship was in desperate need of cleaning and the dust tickled their noses.

The following day a small convoy made up of the *Bloemfontein*, the *S.S. Mormacport*, two cargo ships, three destroyers, and two troop boats set sail from Norfolk Naval Base.

The pool area of the ship was now filled with the huge 155-mm artillery guns. Deck chairs had vanished. Marines had to either lean against the railing or sit on a cargo hatch when they were topside.

Belowdecks, the ship's berths were packed as tightly as the cargo in the holds. The bunks were bolted to the bulkheads four high.

"If you wanted to turn over in your sleep, you had to slide out and then go back onto the bunk the other way," Chuck said.

The decks where the Marines slept were also filled with cigarette smoke as men, most still in their teens, sat around playing cards and smoking. A Marine could get away from the choking smoke during the day. The tangy sea air carried it away. The sea would have carried away the butts, but many Marines simply dropped them on the deck and crushed them out with the toes of their boots, a landlubber's habit.

At night, though, the Marines couldn't smoke on deck for fear that a lighted match or glowing cigarette would give away the convoy's position to an enemy submarine. Marines patrolled topside on blackout watch to ensure no one violated that rule.

After only a night in the four-high bunks choking on smoke and with another Marine's backside nearly pressing into his face, Chuck decided he'd rather sleep up on deck. Not only did he have fresh air, but he could move comfortably. He bedded down near where the landing boats were stowed and slept on top of his lifejacket to provide him some cushioning from the metal deck.

It was quieter topside. Far fewer people were on deck at night and those that were tended to talk quietly, almost as if respecting the night or fearing the Japanese or Germans would somehow hear them. It didn't stop the Marines below deck from making a lot of noise though. Chuck could sometimes hear them through the closed hatches.

Night time was also when the movement of the sea could be felt. As Marines lay still, they were either lulled to sleep by the movement of the ship or they made frequent trips to the latrine as they discovered that they were susceptible to sea sickness. Luckily for Chuck, he was among the former group.

The biggest drawback to sleeping topside was that he could never sleep late in the morning. He had to make sure that he was up early because the first duty of the day was for the crew to swab the decks and wash off all of the cigarette butts that had been dropped and crushed on the deck from the previous day.

During the first days of the journey, the Marines didn't know where they were headed. They had been ordered to board the ship at Norfolk and they had done so. The *Bloemfontein* had headed due east of out Norfolk and Chuck thought that they might be heading to fight in Europe. The Marines were using old French artillery pieces and Chuck even had a fleeting hope that they might be going to France to return the worn-out guns since he had no love for them. They were clumsy to use, hard to aim, and finicky to maintain.

The *Bloemfontein's* eastward heading soon changed, and in the mornings, the sun rose off to Chuck's left and in the evenings, it set off to his right. They had turned south. That meant that they would be stationed in the Pacific Theater somewhere, though no one knew exactly where.

The stories of the fighting with the Japanese among the Pacific islands was not encouraging as to what the Marines would find when they arrived. The United States had recently won the Battle of Midway in June, but they had lost at Wake Island and the Battle of the Coral Sea. The Marines had taken heavy casualties at all of those battles.

"I was sure one of the reasons we had had so little training was that they needed us to fill all of the holes in the units," Chuck said.

In other words, he believed that the new Marines would be cannon fodder. Surviving would be their real training and the Japanese weren't going to make that easy. The Japanese were swarming over islands throughout the Pacific, taking what they wanted and putting the islanders to work for them as forced labor just as they had done with the Koreans whom they had conquered. The Allies continued to retreat in the face of what seemed an unstoppable army. The Marines were learning, though. Chuck just hoped that he had learned enough at Parris Island to survive the fighting in the Pacific.

The Marines ate twice a day while on their voyage, not that they wanted to eat more. Meals were often poor tasting and poor nutrition like hardtack, Vienna sausages, and grits. The mess lines were long even with four different lines of Marines being served at the same time. Once the food was dumped on their trays, the Marines ate quickly at long tables where they were jammed shoulder to shoulder with other Marines.

"The food was slop," Chuck said. "And the lines were so long, by the time they got finished feeding one battalion, the next one was ready to eat."

They ate little fresh food on the ship, and a lot of that was bad or rancid. When Marines felt sick, they weren't sure whether it was from the rolling waves or the food. One evening the Marines were served veal cutlets, which they enjoyed at first. The meat turned out to be tainted and it started sending the Marines running for the latrine a few hours later.

"By 0100, the whole complement of troops was on the main deck slashing through excrement as much as a foot deep near the outhouses whose drains had plugged long ago. Buddies were taking turns holding each other as they squatted over the ship's rails," according to ... *The Difference: A History of the 5th and 14th Defense Battalions United States Marine Corps*.

It didn't help that the smell of bad food mixed with the scent of hundreds of Marines crammed into a hot, too-small space, and smell of oil burning belowdecks in the engine room.

Between the lousy food and the rolling ship, many of the Marines discovered that they were prone to seasickness. The cesspool and smoke smell below decks didn't help any either. A lot of the Marines spent their days hanging over the railing top side and vomiting into the sea. Those who couldn't make it to an open space on the railing used their helmets.

Other Marines avoided seasickness, but not illness in general from the poor food. They spent a lot of time in the latrine. However, like everything else on the *Bloemfontein,* the latrine barely deserved its name. It was a long water trough with water running through it to carry away waste. For a Marine to use it, he had to drop his trousers and hang his butt over the trough and squat.

With a lot of time on their hands, Marines had to find things to keep them occupied. There didn't seem to be enough space or equipment to exercise properly, though some men did manage a calisthenics program. Some of them played cards and smoked. Some of them would simply lay over a hatch cover topside, enjoying the sun and fresh air. Others would stand at the railing looking out over the ocean and seeing nothing but water for miles and miles in any direction.

The Marines who felt truly sick lined up at the sick bay hatch. They were hoping the Navy doctor could give them quick relief, but the doctor only dosed them with castor oil, which often sent them back to the latrine to vomit.

The Marines one had to watch out for were those who got mischievous when they got bored. Between the rolling ship and running water in the latrine, the trough had small surging waves in it that moved back and forth. Some Marines would time the waves and then set a wad of toilet paper on fire with a lighter or match. Then they would drop the burning toilet paper into the trough at the right moment so the rolling waves would carry it under the bare butt of some unsuspecting Marine and singe him. A Marine's yelp of surprise always brought forth chuckles from nearby Marines and curses and threats from the burned man.

Most Marines did what they could to pass the time, but with so many people crammed together in a relatively small space, tempers tended to grow short from time to time. During one instance, Master Sgt. Elmer Eaton chose to pick on Chuck about his size and courage.

"If you say that you're fifteen, I'll get you out of here," Eaton teased Chuck.

Whether Chuck was having a bad day or he had simply had enough of Eaton's taunting isn't clear. What is clear is that

Eaton said the wrong thing at the wrong time. Chuck spun around and punched Eaton in the face.

Eaton staggered backwards a few steps and rubbed his jaw. Chuck expected either to be hit back or thrown in the brig.

Eaton did neither. He just glared at Chuck and said, "You'll never be more than a private in this outfit."

Then Eaton turned and walked away, leaving Chuck unsure as to whether he was lucky or not. Eaton was right, though. Chuck never did get promoted while serving with Eaton, but whether it was because of Eaton or not is unknown.

Another Marine wasn't so lucky. Francis Marion Ashcroft, who everyone called the Swamp Fox, was caught sleeping on his night watch. He was arrested and tried and found guilty. His sentence was two months of extra policing duty and a reduction in pay of thirty-three dollars a month for two months.

The Panama Canal was sighted around 8 a.m. on the morning of July 13 after a week at sea, and the *Bloemfontein* began to move through, beginning the passage from the Atlantic Ocean to the Pacific Ocean at 11 a.m.

The Panama Canal had opened in 1914, after thirty-two years of false starts and construction. The French had started digging the canal in 1882, but had stopped after running into engineering problems and high mortality from disease. The United States Government realized the value of a canal across Panama during the Spanish-American War as warships from the West Coast of the United States had to travel around the tip of South America and then sail northward before reaching the sites where much of the action of the war took place.

The U.S. government took over the canal project in 1904 and saw it through to completion at a cost of $375 million. Once completed, ships could save nearly 7,900 miles when traveling between coasts by traveling through the canal.

The *Bloemfontein* entered the canal from the north through

Limon Bay near Colon, Panama. The crew allowed a canal pilot to come aboard the ship. It was his job to take the ship safely through the canal, and he served as the ship's captain while the *Bloemfontein* was in the canal. Small locomotive engines called mules—at one time they had actually been mules—ran along either side of the canal connected to the ship by long cables. The locomotives moved along with the ship through the locks pulling the ship along and stabilizing it so that it wouldn't hit the sides of the canal causing damage.

Three locks raised the ship from the Atlantic Ocean to Gatun Lake, a 422-square-kilometer lake. As the *Bloemfontein* moved into each lock, steel doors shut behind it. Valves were then opened that allowed water from Gatun Lake to flow into the lock, slowly raising the ship to the level of the next lock. Once the water in the lock was level with the water level in the next lock, gates in front of the ship opened and the locomotives pulled the ship into the next lock.

Coming out of the third lock, the tow cables that connected to the locomotives were disconnected and the *Bloemfontein* sailed across Gatun Lake under its own power with the canal pilot directing operations.

Gatun Lake was created by damming the Chagres River. The Gatun Dam on the south side of the lake was an eighteen-million cubic-foot earthen wall that was second in size to only the Hoover Dam in Nevada and Arizona.

At the southeastern end of the lake, the ship entered the Gaillard Cut, which was almost like being in the canal once again. It was 150 meters wide and thirteen meters deep at its shallowest. It was a thirteen-kilometer-long, man-made passage that kept dredgers busy trying to keep it clear of rock falls and other debris.

Once the ship was through the cut, tow lines were attached to a new set of locomotives to help pull the ship into the Miquel Pedro Locks. The ship was lowered nine meters to the Miraflores Lake. From there, the ship sailed across the lake for two-and-a-half kilometers before entering the Miraflores Locks. This pair of locks lowered the ship to the same level as the Pacific Ocean. Miraflores means "to watch flowers" in Spanish, but no one was watching flowers from the lake or locks. They were watching how the ship moved through the canal.

From this point, the *Bloemfontein* passed through a long channel that took the ship past Balboa and LaBoca until it reached the Bay of Panama, part of the Gulf of Panama on the southern end of the country. The canal pilot left the boat there and the ship was ready to journey into the open seas.

The forty-eight-mile trip took around eight hours. However, before the canal opened, ships had to travel around the southernmost tip of South America via the Strait of Magellan or the Drake Passage, a trip that took weeks longer.

Once the *Bloemfontein* was through the canal on July 15, it docked near Panama City for the night. Chuck had stayed awake and on deck during the canal passage so that he wouldn't miss seeing anything. Part of the reason was his fascination at seeing how the canal worked. The other part of the reason was that it was something different to look at other than water.

As the ship had passed through the canal, Chuck had seen barrage balloons floating in the sky to provide some protection to the ships in the canal and early warning of any attack from enemy aircraft. Destroying the canal would have slowed the America's ability to get troops into the Pacific from the Atlantic and vice versa. It was a tempting military target.

After leaving Panama City and heading south, the Marines were told that their destination was Auckland, New Zealand.

The following morning all of the men were given shots. They lined up with their arms exposed, as if their shoulders hadn't been stabbed by enough needles at Parris Island.

Whether it was a reaction to the shots or simply their poor diet, most of the Marines came down with dysentery. The men were so miserable and so weak that it was hard enough to stay squatting over the latrine trough that no one played any pranks to burn butts.

On July 17, the *Bloemfontein* crossed the equator at 2 p.m. The first time a person sails across the equator is a special event for sailors and the *Bloemfontein* was carrying thousands of Pollywogs, the term for someone who has never sailed across the equator.

The origins of the crossing ceremony are lost to history, but it was known as far back as the 1500s. Each ship performs the ceremony differently. The basics are that when a ship crossed the equator, King Neptune boards the ship to judge whether the slimy Pollywogs are impersonating sailors or had proven themselves to the God of the Oceans.

To prove themselves worthy to Neptune, the Pollywogs are tested. On the *Bloemfontein,* this involved drinking "poison". Chuck still doesn't know what it was he drank to this day, only that it was "some kind of ugly foaming drink." The Marines also had to crawl through slime spread on the deck while being beat on their backs with wet towels. The repeated dull slaps left Chuck's back looking bright red as if he had been sunburned.

Once the gauntlet was run, though, the Marines were given a large, colorful certificate marking that they were now Shellbacks, trusted seamen and Sons of Neptune. They had become veterans, at least as far as crossing the equator was concerned.

The *Bloemfontein* arrived at Bora Bora in the Society Islands, which are part of French Polynesia, on Sunday morning, July 26. In the center of the island is an extinct volcano that rises more than 2,300 feet in two peaks. The island itself is surrounded by a lagoon and barrier reef.

The United States military had built an air strip, oil depot, and seaplane base to turn the island into a military supply base.

Since that would also make it a possible target for Japanese attack, fortifications were also built. The high peaks on the island gave artillery emplacements a strategic position.

Once the ship docked to take on supplies, the Marines were able to go ashore for a few hours. Chuck enjoyed feeling hard ground under his feet and the chance to eat some decent food. He also visited with the natives on the island. A native girl with dark hair and olive skin wove a flower lei and then placed it over his head before he reboarded the *Bloemfontein*.

Although July had nearly ended, the Marines were now south of the equator where July was winter. It felt that way, too. Chuck and the others started wearing their greens to try and stay warm. For Chuck, it was the first time since April that he had had to put on his greens.

On August 3, the ship docked at Wellington, New Zealand, and the Marines were granted liberty at 5 p.m. They rushed to get off the ship as quick as they could.

"My worst memories of my time in the service wasn't the islands or combat," Chuck recalls. "It was on that *ship*."

The Marines had work to do the next couple of days offloading the *Bloemfontein*, alongside New Zealand stevedores. The stevedores were hard workers, by and large, except for one incident. Chuck's unit had four 155-mm Long Tom artillery pieces. They could fire 100-pound shells more than thirteen miles. However, each gun weighed almost 31,000 pounds, and while the stevedores were lifting one of the guns off of the ship with a crane, it slipped and fell to the dock. The barrel cracked and put the piece out of commission.

When the work day ended at 4 p.m., the men headed into town on liberty. Good chow was a top priority for many of the Marines, and they sought out steak and ice cream. Chuck enjoyed his time in Wellington and thought the people were wonderful. He spent a lot of time on Lambton Quay enjoying the pubs and cabarets along Wellington's commercial district. At night, with all of the city's lights on, it sparkled with life. He considered the food "a treat after the slop, water rations and stinking holds on the Dutch scow." The dishes tended to be Māori using local vegetables like kūmara, taro, and tī, but there were also English dishes due to the influence of Europeans in New Zealand since the late eighteenth century.

"The girls were friendly, elated in most instances, to see the 'Yank,'" Hennessey wrote. "Every third day we had liberty; time to meet more girls, go to the movies, eat and just get hyper of the most mundane things. Red Cross activities, dances, even the temptation of drink was present."

Offloading a ship at the docks at Wellington. Courtesy of Chuck Caldwell.

After ten days in Wellington, the Fifth Defense Battalion headed north to Camp Paekakariki, which in Maori means "perching place of the green parrot." The camp was thirty miles north of Wellington in the hills. The trip took more than an hour by train. The camp had been built on an old golf course in June and could house up to 2,400 men. It was quite a change from the battalion's first station. The Fifth Defense Battalion had organized in Charleston, S. C., on June 16, 1941, and then shipped out to Iceland. They had been stationed there until returning to the states to add the new Marines at Parris Island, one of which had been Chuck.

The Marines lived in tents with stoves that were lit at night to get them warm during the cold winter nights. Although the thermometers said the temperatures never got below freezing, the wind blowing through the camp made it feel much colder. In the mornings, the Marines would rush through the camp trying not to freeze before they reached the shower building, which was made of brick that helped hold in the steam from the hot showers keeping the building warm. The camp food was great even if the weather was miserable. Chuck could eat all of the mutton steaks and eggs he wanted.

"We could have it three times a day if we wanted," Chuck said. "I never tired of it, especially after what I had eaten on the ship."

Training continued at Camp Paekakariki with field hikes, marksmanship training, and squad tactics. It was rough work, particularly since they hadn't trained for a month. Chuck and the other Marines still had fun at times. On August 16, Chuck was on a hike when his squad decided to try and catch one of the sheep that were so abundant in the hills. They chased the sheep, trying to corner one or chase one into the arms of another Marine. The nimble creatures always managed to evade the Marines, leaving them hot, sweaty, and empty handed. Then later in the afternoon, he hitchhiked back to Wellington.

A few days later, the Marines packed their seabags once again. They left Camp Paekakariki on August 21 and rode the train into Wellington. They marched through Wellington in the early afternoon and back to the docks by Lambton Quay. To their relief, the *Bloemfontein* had sailed off to bring misery to another group of servicemen. They boarded the *U.S.S. Libra*, a new Arcturus-class attack cargo ship that had been commissioned in May, and began making ready to sail, which took until nearly midnight.

U.S. Marines drop their kit after reaching their camp at Paekakariki. Courtesy of the Alexander Turnbull Library, F 32257.

Four batteries of the Fifth Defense (F, G, H, and I) were renamed the 290A Detachment along with the Third Barrage Balloon unit and left quickly on the *U.S.S. Fuller*, a Heywood-class attack transport, headed for Tulagi, a small island in the Solomon Islands. Chuck's group spent two days loading the *Libra*, but they finally got to go into Wellington and enjoy a final liberty on August 23. By this time, Chuck and the other Marines had taken a shine to the local girls and didn't want to say goodbye.

The *Libra* left New Zealand on the morning of August 26. It was cold and the sea was stormy, which didn't seem to bode well, but a least the food was better; not as good as it had been in Wellington, but it was a far sight better than it had been on the *Bloemfontein*.

The weather stayed bad for a couple days, and the Marines stayed belowdeck as much as possible. By the time they anchored at Noumea at New Caledonia, it was warmer and the sun was shining.

Chuck volunteered to be part of the work party of fifty or so Marines, partly so he could get ashore. The island was French territory and the headquarters of the U.S. military in the South Pacific. The island had a tropical climate typical of Pacific islands, but it stank of sulfur. What disturbed him, though, was when he saw some of the casualties of the fighting in the Solomon Islands. That was where his battery had been told they were heading and where the rest of the Fifth Marine Defense already was.

The Marines left Noumea on September 1 as part of a convoy of seven transport ships and two destroyers. Out at sea, part of the convoy broke off and headed in a different direction.

The *Libra* arrived at Tongotabu in the Tonga Islands late in the afternoon of the September 5. It soon became a popular port as twenty cruisers and transports arrived the following morning.

Chuck's ship became part of a convoy of vessels that headed for New Hebrides. They arrived at the city of Esperitu Santo, the largest island in the New Hebrides archipelago, on September 10. They were only in port for a few hours before they moved out into the ocean because of an expected air raid from the Japanese.

By September 15, the *Libra* was back at Noumea. For the next ten days, the Marines enjoyed relatively light duty with a lot of entertainment. They had parties, listened to records, swam, and even watched a movie aboard the *U.S.S. President Adams*. In between the fun activities, the Marines hiked to keep in shape.

The Marines left Noumea on September 26 as part of a six-ship convoy. Chuck suddenly found himself busy on gun watch and chow duty. He was only able to catch about four hours sleep, by his estimate, in three days.

The *Libra* landed at Funafuti, an atoll in the Ellice Islands, on October 4. The Marines were expecting the Japanese to either already be in the area or be moving toward it. It was known that the enemy had made extensive aerial reconnaissance of Funafuti in late September.

Funafuti had recently had some excitement, but it was good news, not a battle.

Capt. Edward "Eddie" Rickenbacker was a celebrity by the time World War II started. He had become famous as a race car driver before World War I and then became the United States' top-scoring fighter ace and a Medal of Honor recipient during the war. Between the World Wars he had become the president of Eastern Airlines.

In 1942, Rickenbacker was flying to the Pacific theater as a non-military observer to evaluate the status of the U.S. Army Air Force. His group left Hawaii on October 21 bound for Canton Island. Somehow they became lost in the Pacific and the crew had to eventually ditch the plane in the ocean when it ran low on fuel.

The crew survived seventeen days in life rafts, hoping for rescue as their supplies dwindled and their fresh water ran out. "The men even experimented with saving their urine, hoping the heat and air would somehow distill it enough so that they could drink it. That did not work," according to an article on HistoryNet.com.

They began seeing planes on the seventeenth day, but they were too far away to spot the small life rafts in the ocean.

On the twentieth day, Capt. William Cherry, Jr., who had been the plane's pilot decided to take the smallest of the five life rafts and paddle off, hoping to find land. With no other options, the group decided to allow him to leave. Later, two other men decided they would take another raft and set off in a different direction.

Two floatplanes finally spotted Rickenbacker and the remaining men on the twenty-first day floating on the ocean. The planes had to leave because they were low on fuel, but they soon returned along with a P.T. boat trailing behind them.

Capt. Cherry had been spotted the day before about twenty-five miles away. He was the one who had pointed the Navy in the direction of the rest of the group. The other men had been spotted and rescued as well.

The survivors were taken to Funafuti to be treated at a hospital. When they arrived, they were given a hero's welcome.

Chuck worried as he approached Funafuti. The Marines were expecting to fight on the island and it would be Chuck's first battle. He had heard what the Japanese army and navy could do, but he hadn't seen it firsthand.

Although this is what he had trained for, he still couldn't be sure of how he would react until the time came. No one thought he would run at the sight of danger, but Americans had done it. Marines had done it. Men like him had failed, so why not him?

The Marines found no Japanese on Funafuti. They only found sand, palm trees, 400 natives, and heavy rain.

It was in this heavy rain that the Marines had to unload their supplies and anti-aircraft guns from the *Libra*. Chuck and the other Marines worked through the night. He made fifteen trips back and forth to the ship, each time weighed down by a heavy load.

The natives on the atoll helped out, but it became a competition between them and the Marines to show who was the strongest.

"Ellice natives, to show their strength, would have us load

an ammo box on each shoulder, they'd sink inches into the sand and proudly stagger up the beach to stake their load, saving us a bunch of work," Chuck wrote in his journal.

Besides supplies, about half of the Fifth Marine Defense remained on Funafuti to hold it, but Chuck wasn't one of them. After working almost twenty-nine hours straight unloading the ship, the only place Chuck was going was to his bunk. He fell into it and was asleep almost immediately. He slept from noon on October 3 to 7:30 a.m. on October 4.

The *Libra* left that afternoon, heading to Noumea for the third time. The multiple trips to Noumea were because it was being used as a supply base and hospital. Ships could come into port and resupply before heading off toward another island. The fighting on Guadalcanal had started in August and the military was building up its supplies on Noumea.

At Noumea, Chuck pulled duty in the holds carrying 155-mm shells that weighed ninety-eight to 102 pounds each.

The Marines held the shells by a wooden dowel stuck through a carrying ring. The Marine carrying the shell then had to scale vertical ladders to climb out of the holds. They sweated in 100-degree heat, which plastered their shirts to their bodies. Since he could use only one hand to climb, Chuck had to let go of the rung and grab the next-highest one before the weight of the shell pulled him off the ladder and sent him tumbling back into the hold.

"One round dropped would have wiped out every man below on that ladder," Chuck wrote in his diary.

The Marines stacked the shells topside. They paused to catch their breath and hoped for a breeze off the ocean to cool them a bit before they walked across the deck and climbed three decks down back into the hold.

Once the *Libra* had been off loaded with all of the supplies and equipment that the Marines needed, they boarded the *U.S.S. Heywood.*

The Marines got liberty on October 14 and went ashore to enjoy some swimming. Though enjoyable, the sight of the hospital on the hill that cared for Allied casualties and the large nearby cemetery that showed how often the doctors at the hospital hadn't been able to help was a sobering sight to Chuck.

The *Libra* left Noumea on October 22 in a convoy that included a K22 and a stack "Raider" Destroyer. The ships made brief stops at Esperitu Santo and Efate in New Hebrides. At the latter stop, they moved all of their gear to the *U.S.S. Fuller*.

On October 31, the *Fuller* arrived in the Solomon Islands. The Marines slept topside that night with all of their gear beside them. They needed to be able to go over the side of the ship quickly if they ran into trouble.

Trouble came the following day when they arrived at Guadalcanal.

1942–1943 GUADALCANAL

While Marines had been fighting and dying on Guadalcanal, Chuck and the Marines of the Fifth Defense Battalion had generally been island hopping around the Pacific Ocean and seeing no action. From time to time, Chuck would hear news of the first American offensive against the Japanese. Luckily, he wasn't hearing the mounting casualty numbers from the fighting or he might have started to doubt himself.

Guadalcanal was a small island populated with native villages that were often visited by missionaries. It also had a Lever Brothers coconut plantation.

One Marine described the island as paradise; "the delicious sparkling tropical sea, the long beautiful beach, the minute palms of the copra plantation waving in the sea breeze, the dark band of jungle, and the dun mass and power of the mountains rising behind it to rocky peaks."

While offering no military threat, Guadalcanal was in a strategic location. The Japanese invaded the island and took it from the British in June of 1942. They then shipped in Korean prisoners whom they set to work building an airfield in the jungle. The Japanese intended to use it to penetrate further into the Pacific with their planes, attacking the Solomon Islands and the shipping lanes to Australia.

The Marines first landed on Guadalcanal on August 7, 1942. Although Guadalcanal had 2,047 square miles of land, the Marines' focus had been to hold the few square miles around the air field that the Japanese were trying to finish. The landing had been a major undertaking with seventy-five ships, including four aircraft carriers. The Marines captured the airfield with relative ease, but holding onto it was much harder.

The Japanese, who had been on the offensive since their attack on Pearl Harbor, weren't going to leave the island or the air field so easily. They began sending additional troops to join the fight. The Marine Corps recalled the First Raider Battalion and the First Parachute Battalion from Tulagi and Gavutu and placed them in reserve near the air field, which had been renamed Henderson Air Field in honor of a Marine Major Lofton Henderson, who was the first Marine aviator to die at the Battle of Midway.

In the days after the initial Marine landing, the Japanese launched a counterattack with seven cruisers and one destroyer. The Japanese surprised the Allies and during a night battle, sank four cruisers while only taking light damage.

The surprise attack forced the American ships to withdraw before they had unloaded supplies for the Marines on Guadalcanal. This left them with limited supplies and food with which to fight their battle and no naval support.

Chuck was among the Marines who criticized the Navy, and in particular, Admiral Jack Fletcher, for this debacle called the Battle of Savo Bay. Not only did the withdrawal of the Navy task force leave the Marines ashore unprotected, the carriers were too far away to help the other Navy ships during the battle. By mid-October, Fletcher was replaced by Admiral William "Bull" Halsey, who had a "go get 'em, take no prisoners" approach that the Marines appreciated. Halsey actually relieved Vice Adm. Robert L. Ghormley as commander of the South Pacific Area, but that gave him control over the U.S. forces at Guadalcanal as well.

The Raiders, an elite Marine unit that specialized in aquatic light-infantry combat, conducted two raids to put the Japanese on defense and relieve some of the pressure on the Allied troops around the air field. The first raid was on Savo Island, but when the Raiders arrived they found that the Japanese had already left.

The second raid was launched against the Japanese supply base on Tasimboko. The Marines destroyed several Japanese artillery pieces and a large cache of supplies, disrupting the supply line to the Japanese soldiers on Guadalcanal. Just as importantly, it also yielded intelligence about the Japanese forces on Guadalcanal.

The Marines used the intelligence to mislead Japanese forces while shoring up areas where it looked like the Japanese planned to attack.

On September 12, 1942, more than 2,000 Japanese soldiers attacked the southern side of Henderson Field. They believed that it was lightly defended and would be easy to break through, particularly with an overwhelming force. At one time that might have been true, but the Marines knew about the Japanese plan and had reinforced the defenses. The Japanese attacked entrenched Marines. Even so, they still outnumbered the Marines three to one.

The Japanese cruisers and destroyers shelled the area with the intention of softening up the American defenses. Japanese General Kiyotaki Kawaguchi began making probing attacks that emphasized their strength in numbers and attempted to isolate small groups of Marines so they could be overwhelmed. Fifty of the Raiders were cut off at one point and were forced to withdraw from the fighting. At dawn, though, it was the Japanese who broke off their attack and regrouped.

The Marines pulled their line back. This would force the Japanese to cross open ground on their next attack, which they did at nightfall. Unlike previously, this time the Japanese struck everywhere at once and the center of the line buckled.

The Marines pulled back to the last defensive position before Henderson Field and about 300 Marines formed a U-shaped line around the knoll. Some of the men started moving toward the rear, but the officers shouted at them, "Nobody moves, just die in your holes!"

The Japanese continued their advance, swarming around the left flank, but the parachutists launched a counterattack and the line held. Meanwhile, Marine artillery and grenades thrown by entrenched Marines took out scores of the Japanese.

Kawaguchi launched two more attacks on the Marines on September 14. Both failed and the Japanese broke off their attack. While dozens of Marines had fallen, they had taken hundreds of Japanese with them.

Fighting was nearly as fierce in other areas. Marines faced heavy opposition from the Japanese on the west side of the Matanikau River and had to withdraw. The First Battalion, Seventh Marines were nearly annihilated during an amphibious assault.

The Japanese tried an assault on October 7 and were soundly defeated. The Marines captured their assembly and artillery positions on the east bank of the Matanikau.

The surviving Raiders were shipped out to New Caledonia for some much-needed rest.

Nearly half of the Raiders had been killed in fighting on Guadalcanal. Marines were needed to fill in openings created by the resting Marines and the ones who had been killed.

That is where the inexperienced Fifth Defense Battalion with whom Chuck fought, was needed.

The fighting on Guadalcanal had been going on for nearly three months when the *U.S.S. Libra* arrived with more Marines. The *Libra* was an attack cargo ship, but it wasn't often that the first part of its name was put to the test. Now, approaching the ninety-mile-long island, all of the ship's guns were manned. It had four 40-mm guns, eighteen 20-mm guns and a 5-inch/.38-caliber gun. This last was an excellent anti-aircraft gun that could fire fifteen rounds per minute, even more if the crew was well trained.

On November 2, the Marines went over the side of their

ship and climbed down the cargo nets into the Higgins boats that had been lowered to the ocean earlier. Chuck and the other men were packed onto the boats with barely enough room to move around. Few of them spoke. They listened. They listened for commands from their officers. They listened to the water smashing against the sides of the landing craft like slaps across their faces to keep them alert. Most of all, they listened for gunfire. Ahead of him, Chuck could see the white sand beaches pockmarked with craters where shells had exploded.

Marines aboard a Higgins Boat headed toward Guadalcanal. Courtesy of Chuck Caldwell.

The Marines wore grim expressions or blank stares into nothing. A few could be seen moving their lips as they prayed silently. They were going into battle. No doubt about that. Would they live or would they die? Would they fight or would they run? The questions went through the minds of all of the Marines as they approached the island.

No one was calling Guadalcanal a paradise now. The Marines already on the island wrote of the swamps and mosquitoes. It was a "vine-choked rainforest that blocked out the sun, slimy mud, rotting vegetation, damp undergrowth that gives of vile, unforgettable smell, insects, diseases, snakes, scorpions, spiders as big as a man's fist, blue green mountains cut the island lengthwise, coral ridges drop down to the beaches, Kunai grass grows on the ridges, looks beautiful blowing in the breeze, but the blades of the grass cut like a knife and the grass grew so high it sawed at men's throats."

As they neared their landing site, Chuck heard a new sound. The rumble of plane engines mixed amid machine gun fire. Two Marines manned each boat's Browning Automatic Rifles, but they had few targets at which to fire. They looked up and saw Japanese planes attacking them. The *Libra*'s guns fired as did artillery on the island.

Chuck clutched his rifle tighter. The Marines were carrying bolt-action Springfield rifles that were more than twice the age as the average Marine coming ashore. They were the same type of rifles that Chuck had used in the ROTC at the University of Alabama. The semi-automatic M-1 rifles had been introduced in 1936, but they hadn't made their way to the Pacific Theater for general use yet. Each Marine also had a "unit of fire" or a day's worth of ammunition, which would disappear quickly if they came under heavy fire.

They landed in at Red Beach, west of the Ilu River. Oddly, the beach wasn't red. It had white sand. Beyond the sand, they could see dark green palm trees and dense undergrowth that marked where the jungle began.

Hitting the sandy bottom, the Higgins boats stopped in the shallow water and the Marines scrambled over the gunwales.

Once the Marines made it to shore, they ran for the cover of a nearby coconut grove and set up a defensive perimeter, digging trenches and setting up machine guns and mortars. They spent the night there in the pouring rain, watching water pool at the bottom of their trenches. Between the night and the rainfall,

Chuck could barely see in front of himself. The sound of the rain masked any sounds. Few of the Marines could sleep, fueled by adrenaline and a fear that a Japanese soldier was stealthily approaching just beyond sight.

Meanwhile, the Japanese were landing their own troops east of the Marines at Tetere. More than 1,500 of them managed to come ashore in the night.

That first night in combat was a rough one for Chuck. He kept hearing a loud booming going on. He knew that it was artillery fire, and he worried that the Japanese might be zeroing in on the Marines' position. The Marines who had been on the island for a while seemed unconcerned.

How could they be so calm? Had they given up hope of surviving this campaign?

Then one of the "old timers" noticed Chuck's distress and said, "Don't get scared. They're ours."

The next morning, the Marines began pushing toward Henderson Field, which was about a mile away. It was still raining, but at least now they could see something. His artillery crew fired thirty-one rounds into a Japanese village, but he was not sure how much damage that they did.

They took cover during another air raid and even more Japanese landed east of Koli Point, but more Americans were landing, too. The Second Marine Raiders and Eighth Marines landed the following day to even out the numbers somewhat, although the Marines were still outnumbered.

The Marines held their own whether it was on land or air. During one air raid, more than two dozen Japanese bombers protected by zeros made a run against Henderson Field. The Wildcats flown by Marine pilots took to the air to defend the field and engaged the Japanese in a dogfight that lasted more than two hours. Chuck watched a bomber and two zeros get blown out of the sky.

The Japanese air raids came almost daily. A half dozen to a

dozen bombers would fly in low from Japanese ships surrounding the island to drop their bombs. The goal was to destroy the runway on Henderson Field in the hopes of keeping the Marines on the ground.

The raids kept the Marines' nerves on edge, especially at night when they couldn't see the planes coming.

Chuck (right) and a friend pose for a picture on Guadalcanal. Courtesy of Chuck Caldwell.

The Marines dug their fox holes and air raid shelters and considered themselves solidly defended. However, some mornings, they would find odd footprints in camp. They were left by people with fairly small feet about the size of Chuck's but they were neither booted nor barefoot. Someone explained to Chuck that the prints were made by tabis. These were Japanese tennis-shoe-type boots that separated the big toe from the rest of the toes.

Then it dawned on Chuck that the footprints meant that the Japanese had come through their camp unseen. They could have attacked and killed who knows how many Marines, but they had only passed through.

"It made me think that somebody was not guarding our camp too well," Chuck said. "That's when I started sleeping on my back with my K-bar next to me."

On November 7, Chuck saw the growing Marine cemetery on Guadalcanal. It was a cleared area near Henderson Airfield with too many mounds of fresh dirt marking graves. Some of the graves were covered in palm fronds while all of them had a wooden cross with the dog tags of the dead Marine tacked on it at their head. In the center of the cemetery, a raised dais made of logs had been erected for an altar where services to bury the dead were conducted.

It was a sobering sight. Chuck counted over 400 graves with many more in the hills. These were men who would never return home to their families. They had died here on some small island in the Pacific that none of them had probably heard of before they arrived.

As he walked through the site where one of the battles had taken place on the Tenaru River, he saw helmets, packs, rifles, and other equipment left by fallen Japanese.

After a week on the island, Chuck finally found some time to wash his clothes and himself. He went swimming and washed his clothes in the Lunga River. They had to be on watch in the river. Guadalcanal had no alligators, despite having a river called Alligator Creek, but it did have crocodiles that could attack the careless.

One of the other Marines in Chuck's unit was George Noll. He was a nice enough guy but an odd duck. He never wore socks and he let his beard grow out. When the Marines were washing in the river, George would wade in making sure to hold his beard, which was caked with ketchup, crumbs and other things, out of the water. He didn't want to get it wet.

***

Chuck Caldwell's gun crew on an old French 155-mm artillery piece. Courtesy of Chuck Caldwell.

Given how often the Japanese were running air raids, the Marines started building strong air raid shelters. They would dig large, rectangular holes about five feet deep and then roll coconut tree logs over top of them to serve as a roof. Then on top of the logs, the Marines piled a layer of sandbags. It wouldn't stop a direct hit from a bomb, but it would stop a fighter's bullets and bomb debris.

Opposite the entrance a concussion hole was left open. This would allow any concussive force from a bomb exploding a way to pass through the shelter. Otherwise, an explosion would smash against the interior of the shelter and anyone inside. Inside the shelter, dirt seats were carved into the walls for a bit of comfort. It also kept the Marines from having to sit in puddles of water on the ground on rainy days.

Once the shelters were built, the Marines would make a bee line for them whenever the daily air raids occurred.

On November 12, the Japanese made an effort to land more troops at Tassafaronga in seventy-five landing barges. The U.S. Navy ships off shore shelled them as additional Marines attempted to land at other locations on Guadalcanal. The Japanese sent twenty-three bombers and eight zeros to attack the landing Marines. Twenty-eight Wildcats intercepted them and shot down thirty Japanese planes.

Two days later, Chuck was awakened by nearby explosions just after midnight. The Japanese ships had turned their large guns on the island and were shelling it.

"Coconut trees were splintered and falling everywhere," Chuck said.

Chuck piled sandbags around the foxhole where he was sleeping to provide some additional protection. He and George Hardwick had dug their foxholes together in an L shape so that they could talk during air raids. As the shelling continued, Chuck realized that it was too heavy to stay in the foxhole. He needed to get to the air raid shelter.

He started counting how long it was between the time a gun fired and when the shell hit.

One... two... three... four... five... six...seven... one... two... three... four... five... six...seven... one... two... three... four... five... six...seven... The time between firing from the ship and hitting the island was consistent.

When one shell hit nearby, Chuck took off running. Apparently, one of the shells came in quicker than expected. A coconut tree exploded near Chuck, sending wood splinters into his right knee, left chest and wrist.

Chuck yelled as he hit the ground and rolled. He saw blood, but he wasn't feeling pain at the moment. He couldn't rest out in the open. He got to his feet and hobbled on.

"Had I stayed where I was, I probably would have been okay," Chuck said.

He slid into the air raid shelter. He knew that he'd been hit, but he hadn't started hurting yet.

He wasn't alone in the shelter. Other Marines had already gathered there, including George Noll. He had jumped into the shelter half naked. He never slept with his clothes on, only his shivvies. So when the Japanese had started shelling the area, he'd been forced to make a run for safety in his shivvies.

Now the mosquitos were a big problem on Guadalcanal.

"They would get so big sucking on blood that their bodies were nothing but a little bubble of blood," Chuck said.

They were always on the lookout for exposed skin. Not only were they an annoyance, they transmitted malaria, seemingly enthusiastically, to many Marines. Some died from it. Others suffered from bouts of high fever, chills, weakness, headache, sweating, anemia and enlargement of the spleen that would keep them bedridden for weeks.

George could sleep under mosquito netting in his foxhole, but he hadn't been able to bring it with him. The mosquitos were feasting on him. He was slapping at them and cussing at the same time. It served as entertainment for the Marines who watched George jump and roll around, crushing the mosquitos as they tormented him.

"In the morning, he looked worse than me with all of his red mosquito bites," Chuck said.

Early in the morning of November 13, under the cover of darkness, Japanese ships entered the sound between Guadalcanal and Savo Island with the intention of landing more troops on the island. Their intention was to bombard Henderson Field while the Japanese troops landed.

Although the Japanese ships were spotted on radar, the message did not reach Admiral Daniel Callaghan, commander of the U.S. Naval forces, in time and when it did, he wasn't sure of its accuracy.

Once the Japanese and American visually sighted each other's ships, there was confusion at first. Then the two sides opened fire at near point-blank range as the ships crossed paths. At one point, the *U.S.S. San Francisco* accidentally fired at the *U.S.S. Atlanta*.

One war correspondent wrote, "The action was illuminated in brief, blinding flashes by Jap searchlights which were shot out as soon as they were turned on, by muzzle flashes from big guns, by fantastic streams of tracers, and by huge orange-colored explosions as two Jap destroyers and one of our destroyers blew up... From the beach it resembled a door to hell opening and closing... over and over."

The entire battle lasted about forty minutes.

During the battle, the Japanese destroyer *Amatsukaze* hit the *U.S.S. Juneau* with a torpedo while the cruiser was exchanging fire with the Yūdachi. The torpedo broke the *Juneau's* keel and knocked out most of her systems, forcing the Juneau of leave the battle area.

Chuck's artillery gun crew on Guadalcanal. Courtesy of Chuck Caldwell.

The Marines had gone to sleep after the battle ended and when Chuck woke up the next morning, he was feeling the pain from his wounds and sought out a doctor to treat him. He had to settle for a corpsman because all of the doctors had headed for the beach. The corpsman put clean bandages on the wounds and nine stitches in the flesh around his knees.

He hobbled down to see what had drawn off the doctors.

"The beach for hundreds of yards up and down and inland, was covered with thousands of wounded, burned, oil blackened and exhausted sailors and washed-in debris," Chuck said. These were some of the casualties from the early morning battle.

Chuck counted twenty Japanese sailors among those washed into shore. Those who were still alive and conscious were too injured to resist. This was good news because in earlier encounters with Japanese on the island, they had faked being injured in order to shoot Marines who came to help them or even booby trapped themselves so that when their bodies were turned over, a grenade exploded. These Japanese weren't faking, though. They were barely alive.

"I remember seeing one Jap lying on a stretcher; he had a blanket thrown over him and there were no legs. They had packed sand over the stumps to slow the bleeding," Chuck said.

Chuck and other Marines spent the day bringing the wounded water to drink, cigarettes to smoke and C rations to eat.

They began digging trenches, as opposed to foxholes, that faced the north. They were also issued grenades and ammunition for their weapons. Chuck and his gun crew attached their artillery pieces to prime mover tractors and towed them to a position so that they would be able to fire point blank into any Japanese who tried landing on the beach.

The attack didn't come, at least not on land. From their position on the beach, they Marines watched the American and Japanese ships hammering each other with their guns.

Chuck spent part of the following day in sick bay having a doctor check on his wounds. He also asked that his parents not be notified because he didn't want to worry them and he considered his wounds minor. He felt that he'd been hurt worse when the Crimson Tide football players roughhoused with him.

A few days after the big battle, Chuck walked among all of the newly dug graves that held U. S. Marines. He marked where each man was buried and wrote his name down. The list totaled 940 names when he was through.

"They deserved it," Chuck said. "I thought about how easy it could have been for me to be in one of those graves."

Later, Chuck and Harp McGuire hiked to Henderson Field to see how it had fared under the shelling. Harp and Chuck got to be friends and Chuck always thought of Harp as a good singer. Years later, Chuck would be sitting in a movie theater watching Gregory Peck in *On the Beach* when he saw a familiar face.

"I yelled out, 'That's Harp McGuire!' in the middle of the theater," Chuck said.

McGuire had a short film career in the later 1950's and early 1960's before his death in 1966.

As Harp and Chuck crossed the runway, a shot-up torpedo bomber came in. It attempted to land on the runway, but only managed to hit the runway and flip over. However, the three-man crew managed to climb out unhurt.

Thanksgiving Day 1942 fell on November 26, which also happened to be Chuck's nineteenth birthday. He spent his birthday washing up in the Lunga River and eating ham for dinner.

With the Marines in firm control of the island, supplies became more regular. Food had been scarce at times, particularly for the first Marines that arrived in August. Guadalcanal seemed to have little to offer either. Some Marines harvested coconuts and others found bananas, but there was no game to hunt unless you wanted to cook an iguana.

The Marines had captured a large Japanese warehouse at Henderson Field filled with rice and tins of fish. They supplemented their C rations with that to get through the lean times.

Days fell into a series of air raids and some ground action. It reached the point where the Marines could even recognize some of the planes attacking them. "Washing Machine Charlie" flew a plane with engines that made an unsynchronized hum that the Marines came to recognize.

What may have caused the most damage was disease. Marines were coming down with dysentery and malaria. To try and combat it, they were being issued Atabrine tablets each day.

In early December, the First Marines left and were replaced with U.S. Army. The Second Marine Raiders left mid-month. The shift in forces in the island also meant a change in command. General Alexander Vandergrift turned over command of the U.S. forces on the island to Army General Alexander Patch on December 9. Marines would still have a presence on Guadalcanal, but they were slowly being sent elsewhere even as the number of soldiers increased.

Chuck got to see both generals one evening unexpectedly. He and his buddy, Wayne Pense, were heading back to their camp when the Japanese began an air raid. They jumped into the first covered air raid shelter that they saw.

When Chuck looked up he saw a table at the other end of the shelter and General Vandergrift sitting there with an army general that Chuck didn't recognize. He only found out later that it was General Patch.

Neither general said anything to the startled Marines. Chuck and Wayne stood up and hurried out as quickly as they had come in.

Chuck (standing, in the center) and fellow Marines on Guadalcanal. Courtesy of Chuck Caldwell.

Up to this point, Chuck's battalion had stayed near Henderson Field. They had been warned to stay away from the Cavo Range because headhunters lived there.

"We were told not to go into those mountains because those guys are liable to kill you. I said, 'What do you think the Japanese are trying to do?'" Chuck said.

Chuck never did see any headhunters. He imagined them just sitting up in the hills watching the "civilized" people kill each other. The only natives he saw were sitting around chewing betel nuts. The juice from the nuts gave them a purple or red smile. The seed came from a type of palm tree. It was chewed the way Americans chew tobacco and it was just as addictive.

During one excursion, Chuck's artillery crew was sent off north of Henderson Field to Koli Point to support the Seventh Marines who were fighting the Japanese there. The Marines had been warned that if they were captured by the Japanese, they were likely to be tortured before they were killed.

"We were warned, but we had it proved to us," Chuck said. "Moving out to Koli Point, we passed a native village where the Japanese had beheaded two nuns."

Spotters from aircraft radioed information to the artillery. Chuck and his crew used the information to target a Japanese village where ammunition and food was being stockpiled to support the remaining Japanese troops on the island. This was Chuck's first combat firing of his artillery gun and his crew wiped out the village.

The mail caught up with Chuck on December 17. He got a package and seventeen letters that helped cheer him up amid air raids and shelling back and forth. The mail helped Chuck hold onto his sanity, unfortunately, the same couldn't be said for the camp cook who simply lost it one night.

Like many enlisted men, Chuck had no love for a lot of the officers. He was particularly upset after Zale Rains died from black water fever, which is another name for cerebral malaria.

"He was a good ol' boy from West Virginia who had wounds on his back from where his ex-wife shot him with buck shot as he was running away from her," Chuck said.

Zale had been in the hospital for his illness. As soon as he was sent back to the unit, he was put in a work party filling sandbags in 110-degree heat. He quickly relapsed and died. He was the only person on Guadalcanal to die from black water fever. Chuck and many other men blamed the officers, many of whom they saw as uncaring and incompetent for Zale's death.

On Christmas Day, the Marines had a special meal of turkey, French fries, dressing, gravy pudding, celery, olives, ice tea, apples, oranges, bread, butter, jelly, nuts, and hard candy. Chuck enjoyed the meal, which is something he couldn't often say about Marine chow.

"If it wasn't for red lead, most of it would be inedible," Chuck said. Red lead was what the Marines called ketchup.

The Marines had taken to eating two meals a day at 9 a.m. and 4 p.m. This was to avoid the air raids that the Japanese made during what they had assumed were the Marines' meal times for breakfast, lunch and dinner.

He also got a Christmas package from his parents and one from his sister and her husband, Tom. The package from his parents contained homemade cookies, which he enjoyed.

By the end of December, it was estimated that only a few thousand Japanese remained on Guadalcanal. Those who hadn't been killed or captured in the ground actions, were being removed. However, even after Secretary of the Navy William "Frank" Knox declared that the Solomon Islands were secured, there was still fighting going on and still Marines dying.

The same day that Chuck heard that the islands were secured, he watched ambulances taking wounded Marines to the hospital. They had been injured in fighting around Hill 27, Hill 31, and Grassy Knoll.

The new year continued much the same as the old one had. Ground fighting was minimal, but there were still near daily air raids. Also, while it may have been January, the temperatures at Guadalcanal could still climb to more than 120 degrees.

However, while the Japanese had backed off somewhat, they weren't ready to give up the island entirely. The night of January 14 into January 15, there was heavy bombing of the island. The Japanese bombers dropped bombs in a line along the beach.

"Had they dropped one more bomb, it would have been in our camp," Chuck said.

He knew this because he walked off the bombing pattern,

measuring the gap between the bombs. One of the bombs had dropped alongside a ridge pole in a tent occupied by six 164th Infantry soldiers on the beach. It was a daisy cutter that went off a foot from the ground and killed five of the soldiers.

"There were bits of jaw with teeth, fingers, etc. The grass surrounding the tent was laid back out from the tent center pole which was only a two inch stub of wood. The sixth man who had only gotten his legs over the side of his cot had these legs neatly blown off," Chuck said.

The Army continued to ship men in to replace Marines who were being sent elsewhere.

On January 21, the Marines and soldiers endured the longest air raid on the island to date. So much for having control of the Solomon Islands. The first raid lasted an hour and a half. There was a half an hour break before the bombing began again, and this time it lasted seven hours. While the spotlights could reach the aircraft, the anti-aircraft guns couldn't.

This marked the beginning of some long air raids against the Americans on the island. It reached a point where the Japanese must have felt they could bomb at will.

"These damn Japs are getting awfully bold of late," Chuck wrote in his journal. "They sent their bombers over at high noon."

By the beginning of February, the Marines and Army believed that the Japanese were going to try landing on the island once more. The night of February 1 was spent manning guns in anticipation of an attack. Additional Army and Marine units were rushed from inland to help reinforce the American positions on the beach. Some Japanese did land, but they were west of Chuck's position and they were routed by late morning.

Despite all of the bombing runs, Chuck's camp had never been hit by one in his three months on the island. On February 3, a 500-pound bomb dropped on the camp and destroyed two tents, but amazingly, no one was hit. They were all in their foxholes.

Chuck (second from right, wearing the helmet) and his fellow Marines relaxing on Guadalcanal. Courtesy of Chuck Caldwell.

On February 7, Chuck visited the cemetery on the island where all of the military personnel who had died were buried. By his count, it had more than doubled in size since his unit had moved to the beach in November. He counted three sections, each with thirty-one rows of ten.

They also checked the prison camp set up to hold Japanese prisoners at Point Esperance since it had been reported that the Japanese were trying to remove their troops from the island using submarines. The hundreds of prisoners there would be an attractive target for a rescue.

On February 9, it was announced that all organized Japanese resistance on Guadalcanal had ended.

By mid-February, things began to settle down to the point where the Marines started showing movies at night. The Marines even began to scavenge the former Japanese lines looking for knives, helmets, canteens, etc. to keep as souvenirs. Chuck found a piece of a Japanese zero with the Japanese flag emblem on it and he stowed it away in his seabag.

Around this time, Master Sergeant Elmer Eaton, the Marine whom Chuck had punched on the voyage to New Zealand on the *Bloemfontein*, was promoted to lieutenant. Of course, there were no lieutenant bars available to pin on Easton's lapel so someone came up with the idea of cutting a piece of shell casing into the shape of lieutenant bars and pinned it to his shirt. It was done in front of the company and looked quite comical and some of the Marines laughed.

Not Chuck. He wasn't going to put himself on an officer's bad side any more than he already was.

By March, Chuck was really wishing he had a fresh uniform. His Marine khakis were a patchwork and his dungarees had holes in them.

Near the end of February, the military had to deal with another enemy they couldn't do anything about. A storm came through that caused a tidal wave in the New Hebrides and caused a great storm on Guadalcanal.

"It really bent the palm trees," Chuck wrote. "Around 1800 the rains came and I mean they really came!"

It rained on both February 24 and 25, leaving the island a mud pit. Things that weren't stuck in the mud were floating in the puddles.

By the beginning of March, Chuck's outfit had been on the island the longest and there was talk that they would be relieved.

Things were settling down on the island, although there was still an air raid every few days. Some days, the Marines even found it quite boring. There wasn't much do if they weren't fighting.

"Our recreation here consists of reading magazines which are passed around, sleeping, eating and talking about home," Chuck wrote.

Things got so bad that the Marines started listening to Radio Tokyo for fun. The Japanese propaganda station broadcast its reports in English, generally using a female announcer that the Marines called Tokyo Rose. The intent was to demoralize the troops with inflated reports of Japanese power and American losses. The Marines could read between the lines, though, and got a sense of what was truly happening.

"We get a kick out of 'Radio Tokyo' every evening at 9. The commentator says things like 'The Imperial Navy had undisputed control of the Pacific.' Then they read letters from captured Aussies and play sad and sentimental music to make us homesick," Chuck wrote.

The propaganda backfired. The Marines listened to it for entertainment.

As the days stretched out, boredom set in. Chuck and the other Marines in his company watched units that had arrived after them leave. They were left to wonder when their turn would come.

On March 22, Chuck learned that the entire First Marine Division and its supporting units were cited by President Roosevelt for outstanding gallantry and determination in capturing and holding the Southeastern Solomon Islands.

The following day, the *U.S.S. Putnam, U.S.S. George Clymer*, and U.S.S. *Fuller* anchored in the harbor. They weren't there to take Chuck's unit off somewhere. They unloaded the 172nd and 137th Infantry to replace the 182nd and Twenty-Sixth Signal Battalions.

It was disappointing not to be leaving, but Chuck and two friends—Ed Rich and Jones—came up with an idea. They gathered up Japanese rifles, knives, and helmets and carried them aboard the *Fuller*. Their goal was to trade them for ice cream to take back to the battery.

The seamen stopped their work to examine the goods while the Marines "drooled" over the cold ice cream. Chuck couldn't remember the last time he had ice cream. He didn't even care what flavor it was. He just wanted to feel the cold run down his throat. The sailors drove a tough bargain and when the Marines went back ashore, they carried only a few cups of ice cream and cakes.

The ships must have attracted the attention of the Japanese. They made an air raid around 8 p.m. that much to the Marines' dismay was successful, at least compared to the Japanese air raids of recent months. The Japanese bombers dropped two bombs and managed to destroy three heavy bombers at Henderson Field.

The fires from the burning bombers acted as a signal for the second wave, which managed to destroy two more bombers.

On March 25, Chuck finally got word that he would be leaving Guadalcanal. However, his anti-aircraft battery was being split into three. A battery would stay on Guadalcanal while B battery (Chuck's) would be taken to Tulagi and C battery would go to Gavutu.

The following evening the Japanese gave Chuck a going-away present. He saw his 109th air raid while on Guadalcanal. It didn't come out one a day but it was roughly six raids a week. On this raid, seven planes made five passes over the island dropping bombs. They killed one person and injured thirteen.

Chuck wasn't going to miss Guadalcanal.

A set of the panels that Chuck Caldwell drew illustrating his time on Guadalcanal. Each panel represents a day from the journal that he kept during his time on the island during WWII. Courtesy of Chuck Caldwell.

1943
TARAWA

When Chuck was finally able to leave Guadalcanal after more than five months on the island fighting Japanese, patrolling, and avoiding air raids, his artillery battery didn't travel too far. The Marines had been told that they were going to get R&R in Wellington. Although things had shifted fairly quickly from the stress of fighting to the boredom of patrolling, the Marines still couldn't relax. Not really. There was work to be done in camp and the threat of a Japanese return to Guadalcanal was ever present.

Wellington gave the Marines something to look forward to. They had enjoyed the hospitality of the New Zealanders and the relaxation of rules that were in effect when they were in camp.

Instead of being shipped off to Wellington, though, Chuck's outfit was taken across the Selar Channel. It was nicknamed Iron Bottom Sound by the Allies because of the number of ships that had been sunk there. They landed at Tulagi, an island to the north of Guadalcanal.

Tulagi was an "almost peanut-shaped island" that was 1,000 yards wide and 4,000 yards long. The one town on the island had "a short street of shops, a cricket field, a small hotel and some bungalows." The town had a Lever Brothers trading post and a small saloon "where fermented coconut juice put men in drunk-heaven." Outside of the town, the island was filled with mountains and "split into chasms; land with dense vegetation."

When the Marines had landed on Tulagi as part of the Guadalcanal invasion in August 1942, they had met fierce resistance. The 900 Japanese troops and Korean laborers who had been on the island when the Marines arrived fought to nearly the last man. Only twenty-three of them had been captured alive when the fighting ended.

Tulagi had an excellent natural harbor that the Allies had turned into a naval base and refueling station. Many of the ships damaged in the fighting around Guadalcanal had anchored at Tulagi for temporary repairs before heading to larger ports for permanent repairs.

P.T. boats used the base for a launching point on missions to stop the Japanese from resupplying their forces on Guadalcanal. "Every evening, at dusk, the roar of three 12-cylinder Packard engines—pushing the PT boats out on patrol duty from the Tulagi harbor could be heard for miles—and I mean—each boat had three 12-cylinder engines," Marine John Hennessey wrote. P.T. 109 was among the P.T. boats that used the harbor. The boat was commanded by Lt. John F. Kennedy, Jr. The boat would be sunk in a collision with the Amagiri on August 2, 1943. Kennedy's actions helped his crew survive the sinking, and after the war, Kennedy entered politics and eventually became President of the United States.

The Marine camp was set up on the side of one of the many hills on the island. They put up their bunks in the dark and then settled down to eat C rations for dinner. They had learned from the days on Guadalcanal when there had been little to eat to appreciate food, even if C rations barely qualified as such.

Their first night on the island it rained throughout the night. Given that it was fall in the Pacific, it was a cold rain. It did wash away the sweat from a hard day of setting up the camp, but it made the trails up the steep hills nearly unclimbable.

"Tulagi seemed to be all hills," Chuck said.

Just when it seemed that the Japanese had given up Guadalcanal, they let the Marines know that they were still around. On April 7, 1943, Japanese Admiral Isoroku Yamamoto ordered an air strike on the island involving almost 400 planes from both the Japanese Army and Navy air forces. It was a larger force than the one that had attacked Pearl Harbor.

"It felt as if the Japanese were following us," Chuck said.

When a coast watcher spotted the Japanese offensive, all available fighters were launched from Guadalcanal. In all, seventy-six fighters took to the air, including Marine Pilot James Swett who had just finished a routine patrol.

Swett was sent to Tulagi Harbor to protect the targets there. Swett served with VMF-221, Marine Air Group Twelve, First Marine Air Wing. He had been a Marine for only a few months longer than Chuck and defending Tulagi during the Japanese raid was his first combat mission.

Swett's division climbed to 15,000 feet.

He heard another pilot on the radio say, "Holy Christ! There's millions of 'em!"

At 17,000 feet, the four planes in his division suddenly faced twenty Japanese Aichi D3A Val dive bombers. As Swett and the other pilots closed on the bombers, they saw Zeroes closing on them from above.

In the ensuing fight, Swett shot down seven Japanese dive bombers and had an unconfirmed eighth kill. Overall, the Americans shot down between twenty-one and thirty-nine planes, depending on whom you asked. Either way it was enough to cripple the impact of the Japanese air raid.

Chuck said the word on Tulagi was that Swett's plane was finally shot down by friendly fire. He must have believed it because when they fished him out of the ocean, he said, "I'm an American. I'm American. Can't you see that?"

While Swett was unsuccessfully trying to stay in the air, Chuck and his team of two other Marines were manning a 20-mm anti-aircraft gun.

Chuck was taking his turn manning the gun when he saw a Japanese dive bomber heading nose first toward one of the many hills of Tulagi.

"I thought that it was crashing," Chuck said, "but then it leveled off and came towards me so that I saw that it had fixed landing gear."

Chuck fired off four shots and watched as the plane crashed into the next hill over. He was disappointed because Marines on the other hill collected souvenirs from the dead Japanese. It was the only confirmed kill Chuck had while manning an anti-aircraft gun.

Chuck nearly came through the fighting unscathed, but the anti-aircraft gun locked in the upright position so that it couldn't be used or transported. He and the other two Marines he was with took turns pulling on the barrel trying to get it to break loose.

It wasn't until they were running ram rods through the barrel to clean it later that the Marines' hands started hurting.

"I looked at my hands and they were just complete blisters," Chuck said.

The Marines had pulled at the barrel using their bare hands and burned them on the hot metal. However, because of all of the adrenaline pumping through their bodies and the action going on around them, none of them had noticed the pain at the time.

With the Japanese no longer on Tulagi, the Marines were sent on patrols to Florida Island, the next island to the north where the Allies had a seaplane base. They traveled between islands in motorized rubber rafts. Once on Florida Island, Chuck and the Marines hiked the mountains searching for a Japanese radio station that broadcast from the island. They spent three weeks hiking all over the island without finding the station.

After two months based on Tulagi, the Marines still hadn't received their promised R&R. Instead, Chuck's artillery battery was sent back to Guadalcanal to rejoin A Battery and help protect Henderson Field. They traveled from Tulagi on a P.T. boat commanded by movie actor Robert Montgomery.

Right after A Battery arrived on Guadalcanal, the Japanese launched an air raid of roughly 100 fighters and bombers against the air field.

It only served to reinforce Chuck's earlier feeling that the Japanese were following them. It may also have simply been the luck of A Battery.

"We were the only outfit in the Fifth Defense Battalion that saw combat," Chuck said.

The battalion had started with ten artillery batteries. Four batteries had been sent to Tulagi in September 1942 when there was no fighting going on on the island. Five of the batteries were left at Funafuti in October 1942 when the Fifth Defense Battalion had been on its way to Guadalcanal. That left only Chuck's battery, A Battery, to go to Guadalcanal and fight.

All of their fighting did finally convince the higher ups that A Battery needed rest. They started rotating groups of ten men to New Zealand for ten days of R&R.

When Chuck finally got his time in New Zealand, he once again enjoyed all of the steak and eggs he could eat and the company of pretty girls. He slept when he wanted and didn't worry about Japanese air raids.

The time flew by and Chuck was almost at the end of his leave when he received orders to report to the docks in Wellington. He didn't know why he was going because he still had a couple days before he needed to return to Guadalcanal. He wasn't alone on the train ride from Camp Paekakariki into Wellington. He was accompanied by many other Marines who were members of the Second Marine Division Infantry and some, like Chuck, were members of other units who were wondering why they were on the train.

When Chuck arrived at the docks, he was told that he was being transferred from the Fourteenth Defense Battalion to the Second Division Infantry and he was ordered aboard one of the transports.

Chuck didn't mind being transferred. He considered the Fifth Defense Battalion a poorly run outfit from being renamed to the Fourteenth Defense Battalion for no reason that the Marines could see, to being split up and spread out, to having needed R&R delayed.

"It was the most-misguided outfit in the Marine Corps as far as I'm concerned," Chuck said.

The top brass in the Pacific had been trying to figure out how to take advantage of their first offensive win in the Pacific. One priority was to set up more forward air bases to make it easier for offensive operations to have air support.

The Allies wanted to take the Mariana Islands because that would put them within air range of Japan. The Japanese realized this as well and had heavily fortified the islands. It was decided that an air attack would be needed to weaken those defenses before sending in ground troops.

This meant that the Allies would first need to capture the Marshall Islands, which were northeast of Guadalcanal. While the Japanese didn't have an air base on the Marshall Islands, they had one on the island Betio on the western side of the Tarawa Atoll.

So it became a game of lining up dominos to fall. To be able to bomb Japan, the Marianas Islands needed to be taken, which meant an air base was needed on the Marshall Islands, but first the Japanese air base on Betio had to be taken out.

Rear Admiral Tomanari Saichiro commanded the base on Betio and had been working for a year to improve its defenses. He wanted to be able to stop an invasion before it ever reached the island or at the worst at the beach. He had numerous pill boxes and firing pits built that put the beaches and water in their field of fire. Impressive as the defenses were, they did not extend beyond the beaches. Buildings in the interior of the island did not have firing ports and offered limited fields of fire.

The Second Division Infantry left Wellington on November

1, 1943, and for the next two weeks the convoy made its way around the Pacific Ocean with no apparent destination in sight. All Chuck and the other Marines could do was endure the crowded ships and poor food.

Finally, on November 14, a message from Task Force Commander Rear Admiral Harry Hill made its way from ship to ship: "Give all hands the general picture of projected operation and further details to all who should have this in execution of their duties. This is the first American assault of a strongly defended atoll and with northern attack and covering forces the largest Pacific operation to date."

The Marines were gathered in large groups in rooms belowdecks. The men were crammed in so that the heat of all those bodies turned the room into a sauna that smelled of cigarettes. The shirts and trousers quickly darkened with sweat. They murmured among themselves, knowing something big was about to happen, but not sure what it was.

Then the officers entered the rooms and the Marines fell silent. The officer then followed Admiral Hill's order and explained the mission to Betio in the small, coral atoll of Tarawa.

Few, if any of the Marines had ever heard of the atoll. There was no reason why they should have.

Betio is the largest island in the Tarawa Atoll, but that was not saying much. The island was only two miles long and 800 yards wide at its widest point. Seen from above, the Tarawa Atoll is roughly shaped like a triangle with Betio taking up the lower left corner.

The Japanese had been working for more than a year to fortify the island. At one point, the 1,247 men of the 111th Pioneers, similar to the Seabees of the U.S. Navy, along with the 970 men of the Fourth Fleet's construction battalion were brought in. Approximately 1,200 of the men were Korean forced laborers. The Third Special Base Defense Force assigned to Tarawa had a strength of 1,112 men. They were reinforced by the Seventh Sasebo Special Naval Landing Force, with a strength of 1,497 men. It was commanded by Commander Takeo Sugai. This unit also had light tanks commanded by Ensign Ohtani.

To overcome this massive defensive force of the island, the Americans had assembled the largest invasion force yet for operations in the Pacific. It included seventeen aircraft carriers, twelve battleships, eight heavy cruisers, four light cruisers, sixty-six destroyers, and thirty-six transport ships. On board all of those ships were about 35,000 troops.

Even news of the impending battle did little to change the tedium of life on the transport ships. They played hand after hand of cards and any reading material on board was passed among hundreds of hands as it was read and reread.

"One methodical Marine tabulated his activities in the nineteen days at sea before the invasion like this:

"Played 215 consecutive games of gin rummy.

"Bought and smoked six cartons of cigarettes and one box of cigars.

"Drank 93 cups of coffee.

"Obtained one crew haircut.

"Washed same pair of sox and same underwear 11 different times.

"Read one Pocket History of the United States.

"Read two religious essays.

"Read 19 mystery stories and one something-or-other called The Haunted Pajamas."

The only noticeable changed came as D-Day neared. The men did less casual activities and more work sharpening their knives and cleaning their rifles.

The naval convoy reached Betio in the early hours of November 20. Reveille sounded at 3:45 a.m. and the Marines rose and made themselves ready for battle. Topside, the Higgins boats and other landing craft were lowered into the water.

The moon was at quarter and few stars shone in the sky.

As the sky began to lighten near 6 a.m., the Japanese watchers saw the ships at anchor miles away and opened fire. The battleships, *U.S.S. Colorado* and *U.S.S. Maryland*, returned fire. One shell penetrated the ammunition storage for one of the Japanese guns, igniting a huge explosion as the ordnance went up in a massive fireball. Three of the four guns were knocked out in short order. Though all four guns fell silent, one continued intermittent, though inaccurate, fire through the second day.

Chuck waited with other Marines on his ship, checking and re-checking his rifle to make sure that it was ready. The repetitive moves to disassemble, clean, and reassemble his rifle helped calm Chuck's nerves even as the explosion of shells landing on water and land shattered his calm.

The Marines then bombarded the island from the air. It was followed by a naval bombardment that lasted another three hours. While the Japanese were being softened up by the bombardment and taking cover, two mine sweepers entered the lagoon and cleared it of mines.

Around 7:45 a.m., a destroyer reported that one of its engines had been hit and was out of commission. It was the first naval casualty of the campaign.

The American plan was to land Marines on the north side of the island in three groups.

Red Beach One ran from the western curve of the island to roughly halfway to the pier that jutted out into the lagoon. The pier was made of white coral sand held in place by coconut tree logs. Red Beach Two began where Red Beach One ended and ran to the right side of the pier. From the left side of the pier to a point that corresponded to the end of the Japanese airstrip was Red Beach Three. Green Beach was designated a contingency landing beach along the western shoreline.

Chuck's group would be going in at Red Beach Two as a reserve unit. The Marines in Chuck's group clambered over the ship's rail and climbed down into the waiting Higgins boats. This was not an easy feat. The Higgins boat would move up and down in the sea while Marines hung swaying from cargo nets with eighty pounds of equipment on their backs. A misstep could send them into sea or get them caught between the Higgins boat and the ship.

Marines boarding landing craft prior to the Battle of Tarawa. Courtesy of the United States Marine Corps History Division.

The landing began at 9 a.m. when the naval bombardment ended, but they soon ran into trouble because the tide wasn't high enough for the Higgins boats to clear the reef. Higgins boats were shallow-draft powerboats, but the battle planners hadn't considered the neap tide on the island. They had planned for high tide to allow five feet of water over the reef, which would allow the Higgins boats, which had a four-foot draft room to spare as they passed over the reef.

Twice a month when the moon is near its first or last quarter, the ocean experiences a neap tide. This happens when the sun counters the pull of the moon. Because of this, the tide doesn't change as much as usual. In this instance, the moon is at its farthest distance from the earth and exerts even less than normal gravitational pull, leaving the waters relatively undisturbed. In essence, there is no tide for two days.

The first waves of amphibious tractors, nicknamed Alligators, reached the reef, climbed over it and continued onto the beach with few casualties. The fourth wave was made up of landing boats and instead of floating over the reef, the Higgins boats got stuck on them.

The boats that were stuck could let their Marines out on the reef. The Marines then started to wade ashore in chest-high water.

However, some boats stopped in deep water to avoid getting stuck on the reef and being a sitting duck for the Japanese guns that were starting to fire heavily again. When one landing boat dropped its ramp, about twenty-five Marines rushed out and into water that was over their heads. "Word was passed back that the water was too deep, so five were dragged back aboard. The remainder hung onto other boat wreckages and made for the end of the pier," according to the book *Betio Beachhead.* Not all of the Marines made it to safety. Some were pulled down too quickly by the weight of their equipment and drowned.

By the time Chuck's group headed ashore, things weren't looking too good for the Marines. They had reached the beaches, but were barely holding that position. Later waves of Marines were taking heavy casualties even before they reached the shore. Ammunition was running low and the Marines were having to scavenge ammunition belts from the dead.

Chuck's group went in on a later wave so they were prepared to wade ashore, but they weren't prepared for the heavier firing from the Japanese. The water was chest deep as the Marines started in toward shore holding their rifles above their heads. As the water grew shallower near the shore, they were able to move faster, but not fast enough. The Japanese peppered the water with bullets. The Japanese had manned their firing pits when the naval bombardment had let up.

Despite enemy fire Marines wade through the surf off Tarawa Island. Landing boats and barges brought them to within five hundred yards of the beach but the coral bottom prevented the boats coming closer to the shore. Courtesy of the United States Marine Corps History Division.

"We lost 300 men in 500 yards," Chuck said.

Chuck tried to ignore the men suddenly floating face down in the water around him. He couldn't, though. He wondered if he dove underwater if he could escape the bullets splashing around him.

"I swam underwater part way and hoped I didn't bring my head up in time to get hit," Chuck said.

Chuck tried to stay low and keep the pier to his left so that it blocked some of the bullets headed in his direction. However, as the depth of the water lessened, it was harder to stay below the edge of the pier.

To make matters worse, when he got to the ramp where Japanese seaplanes were towed out of the water, the beachmaster told him to get up on the pier to off load morphine, ammunition and fresh water from the ships that made it to the pier.

The Japanese seemed to be targeting the Marines on the pier because they weren't firing back. Their hands were full of supplies. As men fell, Chuck walked around them or stepped over them as he carried supplies as fast as he could. Between the heat and his fear, he lost all sense of time.

The Japanese brought up their troops from the southern side of the island to reinforce their troops on the northern side where the fighting was going on. They concentrated their fire on the alligators.

It began to take its toll on the alligators because their hulls weren't heavily armored. A number of the amphibious tractors were stopped in the water. The alligators that did make it over the reef were stopped at the sea wall. Some of the alligators went back to the reef to try and carry men stranded on the Higgins boats, but they had too many holes in them to prove seaworthy.

Marines remained stuck on the reef and pinned down behind the sea wall. Meanwhile, half of the alligators were knocked out of action by the end of the first day.

Two Stuart tanks managed to land on the east end of the beach, but they were quickly knocked out of the action.

At Red Beach Two, LCMs landed and lowered their ramps to allow six tanks to climb over the reef and head to shore. The Marines directed them, but some still got caught in holes caused by the naval bombardment and wound up sinking. The tanks that did make it to shore managed to push the Japanese back 300 yards. However, two more were disabled on the shore; one by a tank trap and another by a magnetic mine. The final tank had its 75-mm gun disabled when a shell hit its barrel.

Other tanks landed, though.

"In those hellish hours, the heroism of the Marines, officers and enlisted men alike, was beyond belief," Richard Johnson, a United Press correspondent, wrote. "Time after time, they unflinchingly charged Japanese positions, ignoring the deadly fire and refusing to halt until wounded beyond human ability to carry on."

Marines working their way to the beach along the pier. Courtesy of the United States Marine Corps History Division.

By noon that first day, the Marines had taken the beach as far as the first line of Japanese defenses. By 3:30 p.m., the Japanese defense line had started to bulge inward in places. By nightfall, the Marines were halfway across the island and only a short distance away from the airfield.

By the end of the first day, Japanese communications were cut off and Rear Admiral Shibazaki, the Japanese commander, was killed. The Japanese units were operating independently. The Marines had managed to get 5,000 Marines ashore with 1,500 casualties. Chuck counted himself among the living, but there was still a lot to do.

He had worked through the day with little rest. Even as night fell, there was work to do. Fires of burning Japanese supply dumps provided enough light that incoming ships could be seen and sometimes targeted by Japanese fire.

That was bad enough and to be expected, but what surprised them is that they were also taking fire from somewhere in the water. It wasn't until 2 a.m. that someone discovered the source of the off shore firing. Japanese snipers were hiding in the hull of a wrecked Japanese tramp steamer. The Marines had to endure the crossfire until daybreak when the Navy bombed it.

The other problem that Chuck and other Marines unloading supplies had to deal with was the pier itself. "The combination of white sand, quarter moon, and blazing background made perfect targets of every man who had to cross its stretch," according to *Betio Beachhead.* "They did so in single file, spaced five feet apart to prevent group slaughter. Stolidly again and again they made the trip with nearly every crossing taking its toll."

The next day, the Marines pushed once more, trying to expand the bulge in the Japanese line. They succeeded and nearly reached Betio's southern shore. Red Beach Two and Red Beach Three ran into new Japanese defenses that had been erected during the night. The machine-gun nests managed to split the Marine forces for a time. By noon, the Marines had set up their own machine-gun nests that managed to take out the

Japanese nests. A few hours later, the Marines had crossed the air field and occupied the abandoned Japanese position.

On the western side of the island, more Marines were landed on Green Beach. They met heavy resistance at first as the Marines taking Red Beach had the day before. A naval bombardment helped reduce the number of pillboxes and gun emplacements. The Marines were able to take this beach quicker and with relatively few losses.

By the end of the second day, the Marines had control of the western end of the island and the airfield.

On the third day, the Marines began strengthening their lines by bringing heavy equipment and tanks ashore at Green Beach. The Japanese were pressed against the southern shore of Betio by the early afternoon. By the end of the day, they were operating in isolated pockets. They tried to mount a counterattack in the evening, but the U.S. artillery fire broke it up.

The following morning, a Japanese submarine sank the aircraft carrier *Liscome Bay*, killing 647 men.

The Japanese continued to try and mount a successful counterattack with banzai charges against the Marines. They continued being pushed back as they came up against artillery, air attacks, naval bombardment, and determined Marines.

The Marines won the day, but there was still small pockets of resistance that needed to be taken care of.

At Red Beach Two, Chuck and the other Marines were exhausted, but they also still had work to do. However, Chuck was alive and unscathed, which is more than could be said for thousands of other men.

"I had two bullet holes in my pants, but no wounds," Chuck said.

However, his malaria had finally shown itself due to his exhaustion wearing him down. Even as the Marines were nearing victory, the world in front of Chuck spun and he collapsed to the pier unconscious.

Marines coming ashore next to the pier on Betio. Courtesy of Chuck Caldwell.

1944
RECOVERY

Chuck spent his return from Tarawa in the sick bay of one of the ships in a destroyer escort. While other Marines celebrated their survival and mourned the fallen, Chuck pulled a blanket tightly around his body and shivered, although thermometers indicated that he was running a high fever. The orderlies tried to keep him hydrated, but he ate very little. His sleep was a series of naps and he lost track of time on the journey from Tarawa to New Zealand.

The important thing was that the Marines had emerged victorious from the four-day battle.

"I spent four days on Tarawa," Chuck said. "We had lost 3,301 men in seventy-six hours."

Of the 3,636 Japanese in the garrison, only one officer and sixteen enlisted men surrendered. Of the 1,200 Korean laborers brought to Tarawa to construct the defenses, only 129 survived. All told, 4,690 of the island's defenders had been killed.

The Second Marine Division suffered 894 killed in action, forty-eight officers and 846 enlisted men. An additional eighty-four of the wounded survivors would soon succumb to what proved to be fatal wounds from the battle. Of these, eight were officers and seventy-six were enlisted men. A further 2,188 men were wounded in the battle, 102 officers and 2,086 men. Of the roughly 12,000 Second Marine Division Marines who had landed on Tarawa, 3,166 officers and enlisted men became casualties.

The heavy casualties created an uproar stateside. While families of the killed were grieving, the public and politicians were asking why so many men had to die for a seemingly unimportant island.

Chuck was unaware of all of this, but he did learn that most of the Marines who survived Tarawa had been sent to Hawaii for R&R. Just off his own much-needed rest in Wellington, Chuck was ready for more and was jealous of those Marines who could enjoy the sun and sandy beaches of Hawaii. Of course, what he didn't learn until weeks later was that those Marines had arrived at a barren camp and had to spend their R&R building the camp.

Although Chuck had collapsed on Betio, he had been wounded—in a manner of speaking—on Guadalcanal. That's where he had contracted malaria along with so many other Marines. Many of those Marines had been sent home after the campaign, while Chuck stayed on. His early symptoms of the disease, which had shown themselves at Guadalcanal had been mild enough to be overlooked. It wasn't until the stress and exhaustion had combined with a malarial attack that felled Chuck that the doctors realized Chuck even had malaria.

Chuck still wasn't sent home, though.

He was shipped to Auckland, New Zealand, and the 1,000-bed MOB4.

MOBs or Mobile Operating Bases had been around since the start of the war. MOB4 had been in Auckland since July 1942.

The U. S. Navy Bureau of Medicine and Surgery had come up with the idea of a prefabricated hospital that could be self-sustaining. The hospital could care for hundreds of patients and had water purification and softening plant; storage spaces for supplies; laundry: mess hall; automotive and ambulance equipment; fire-fighting equipment; light and power supplies; refrigeration facilities; and x-ray, dental, laboratory, and other equipment and facilities of a general hospital.

The MOBs turned out to be not-so mobile. They were useful, though. The facilities weren't a single hospital, but a number of prefabricated huts that could be easily erected. Once set up on a location, they tended to remain there for a long period of time in part, because although the buildings could be taken down and moved, it wasn't always so easy to do that with patients.

The Mobile Operating Base in Auckland provided excellent care. In one report from 1943, more than 4,000 sick and injured servicemen were initially cared for on a hospital ship beginning in August 1942. Two thirds of these men had received previous emergency treatment. Of this number, only seven men died and 368 were transferred to MOB4 where only one died.

Chuck's illness wasn't so severe. He needed lots of bed rest and was treated with quinine until the illness began to subside. After about a week in bed in Auckland, he was given permission to get out of bed and walk around the grounds. Although it was winter when Chuck arrived, the temperatures were still in the upper 50s. He could go outside without too much discomfort.

Auckland was just as beautiful as the rest of New Zealand. The downtown area along the waterfront was filled with shops, restaurants, and artisans. The surrounding area had beaches, mountains, and rainforests.

What helped his recovery more than ever was the nurse the servicemen called the "Angel of Mercy."

"She would go around the hospital and leave little whiskey bottles on the pillows," Chuck said. "It was wonderful."

The hospital had been constructed in the infield of a horse racing track. Chuck liked the look of Auckland just as much as he had Wellington. He couldn't actually go into town to see how it compared, though.

In early January 1944, Chuck knew that he would be transferred out of the hospital soon and he had no desire to go back to the Fifth Defense Battalion, which was now called the Fourteenth Defense Battalion. It had been renamed in January 1943. He thought the outfit was poorly run and couldn't even make up its mind on a name.

He shipped out from the hospital and went to New Caledonia, New Hebrides, and Guadalcanal. He felt like the ship that he was on was just moving from island to island only to take on fuel to go to the next island. While at Camp Kiser on New Caledonia, Chuck volunteered for a parachute battalion, which just so happened to be in the process of being dismantled.

Chuck Caldwell shortly after his release from MOB 4. Courtesy of Chuck Caldwell.

Near the end of January, he was reassigned to the Fourteenth Defense Battalion and shipped back to Guadalcanal. His former artillery battery was still there and hadn't moved while Chuck had fought at Tarawa and spent a couple months in the hospital.

Guadalcanal was securely under U.S. control now so there was very little to do on the island. He drilled on his 155-mm artillery gun, unloaded army ships arriving at Guadalcanal, and trained new Marine replacements.

After a few months of sitting idle on Guadalcanal, Chuck's artillery battery was shipped to Guam on July 21. There had been some fighting here, but by and large, the Marines just went out on routine patrols of the 212 square miles that made up the island. It was the largest and southernmost island in the Mariana Islands and filled with steep cliffs in the north, mountains to the south, and low hills in between.

"There were lots of patrols looking for the Japanese," Chuck said. "We didn't find them, but they found us."

Chuck was on patrol one day when something stung his calf and made him fall. When he checked his leg, he saw that he had a bullet wound that had barely broken the skin. He reached down and pulled the bullet out where it had caught in the material of his pants leg.

"A Japanese sharpshooter must have been so far away that the bullet lost its power by the time it reached me," Chuck said. "I never did see him."

Another Marine was hit four times by the same bullet along his back, but luckily none of the wounds were serious enough to put him in the hospital for too long.

In one instance, the Marines were out hunting for a sailor who failed to report back to his ship. The Marines humped the hills for days, finding nothing. Then one night, Chuck and a squad of Marines were patrolling the coastline along a narrow beach with a high cliff off to their left. Suddenly, his foot caught on what he thought was a tripwire.

He yelled for everyone to freeze.

"In the dark, I realized that I had stepped into the rib cage of a decomposing Jap," Chuck said. "When I realized that there wasn't going to be an explosion, I slowly pulled my foot out."

It took him a long while before he could get another pair of boondockers (boots). The smell of decomposing flesh stayed on the boots and no one wanted to share a tent with him.

During his time on Guam, Chuck also wound up back in the hospital a couple of times when his malaria flared up.

He was in the hospital in November when 2nd Lieutenant Richard Whalen approached him. Whalen had been with the Fourteenth Defense Battalion for a while, but Chuck and another Marine were the only ones who had been with the unit since it left Norfolk. All of the others had been transferred, killed, or shipped stateside.

Whalen told Chuck that the officers had room to send one more Marine home and it came down to Chuck and this other Marine.

"I cut cards for you and you lost," Whalen told him.

Lucky for Chuck, he was shipped out from Guam on November 26, 1944, which also happened to be on his twenty-first birthday. After a few stops, including an eight-day stay at Pearl Harbor, he boarded the *Dancing Wave* and arrived in San Francisco on Christmas Eve and Chuck began a thirty-day leave stateside.

Chuck came back to the United States with sixty dollars to spend, but he had nowhere to go. His train heading home wasn't leaving until New Year's Day. So he and two fellow Marines, Johnny Matthews and Ernie Golden, each bought a fifth of whiskey and decided to go to an all-night theater.

It wasn't that they wanted to watch movies all night, they just wanted to stay warm. Not only were they used to the tropical weather of the Pacific islands, none of them had a coat or jacket. It wasn't something they had needed.

"We ended up with two usherettes who were sisters and the cashier," Chuck said. "We had three Christmas dinners the next day."

But that evening the three Marines took the girls home after they got off work to enjoy a party as Christmas Eve turned into Christmas Day. Chuck was dancing with his date to a Glenn Miller song. Miller was a favorite of Chuck's from his time visiting all of the dance pavilions near Orrville in 1940 and 1941.

"Isn't it too bad we won't hear his band again?" his date asked.

Chuck stopped dancing. "What are you talking about?"

That's when Chuck found out that Miller had been reported missing in action. Chuck had been returning to the states when it happened and hadn't heard the news.

On December 15, 1944, the big-band leader was flying from England to France to play for soldiers stationed there. His small plane disappeared over the English Channel. No sign of Miller or the other two men aboard, Lieutenant Colonel Norman Baessell and pilot John Morgan, was ever found. Theories abound as to what happened from being accidentally brought down by a jettisoned bomb to a failed carburetor, but no one can say for sure what happened, only that a great musician was gone.

The news put a damper on Chuck's Christmas, but when he headed to San Diego later in the day, his mood soon improved. He had to stay in San Diego a few days, but then a sleeper train was chartered just for the Marines who were returning to their homes.

Just like the train that had carried Chuck and other greenies to Parris Island, the seats folded down to create beds for the Marines. The train stopped three times a day to allow the Marines to debark and eat at a restaurant. Chuck saw so many Fred Harvey restaurants that he figured the Marine Corps had a deal with the chain to feed the Marines.

"You would go in the restaurant and there would be nothing but Marines in there," Chuck said. "The waitresses would bring the chow out so that we didn't have to go through the line." He didn't mind, though, he was glad to not be eating Marine chow or C rations.

The sergeant traveling with the train warned the Marines, "When I blow my whistle, you have two minutes to get your ass on the train or you'll be left behind."

Some of the Marines were enjoying their liberty, though, and they didn't want to be rushed. So when the sergeant blew his whistle at the first stop, they took their time finishing up and moving out to the train platform. When they got there, the train was already pulling away from the depot.

Suddenly, this small group of Marines was running down the tracks, chasing after the train and yelling, "Wait! Wait!" They waved their hands in the air holding the liquor bottles they had been drinking from.

Chuck was at the back of the train and saw them running.

"They had been warned," Chuck said. "I was on the train and I just wanted to go home."

At Chicago, Chuck stopped for a day to see his Aunt/Stepgrandmother Alma and her daughters. It was a pleasant visit and the next day, he boarded another train to Cleveland.

When he got off at the station in Cleveland, he was heading for the exit when he saw his parents. They were standing on an overpass where people gathered to watch the riders exiting the train and search for their loved ones. The elevation of the overpass made it easier to spot someone in a crowd.

His parents glanced right over him and didn't wave or register that they had seen him. He wondered if he looked so different after two and a half years in the Pacific that his own parents didn't recognize him. Chuck should have stood out somewhat. Although there were other servicemen and Marines on the train, it wasn't a Marine train like the one to Chicago had been. Marines among the sea of other servicemen tended to stand out.

Chuck walked up the stairs to the overpass and his parents finally recognized him. They hugged him and his mother kissed him before he could even set his seabag down to hug her back.

"I didn't know you had to carry your gun," his mother finally said.

"This is not my gun," Chuck corrected. "It's my Jap rifle."

If his mother had been a boot at Parris Island and had said that, she would have been severely punished by the drill instructor. Rifles were not guns. They were rifles and a Marine's best friend.

However, rather than punish his mother, he simply swept her up in a hug.

The Caldwells had moved from Orrville in April 1942 after Chuck had joined the Marine Corps. George had been offered a job in the defense industry and decided to take it in order to do his part to support his country during a time of war.

The Courier-Crescent had praised George's tenure as the pastor at the First Presbyterian Church in Orrville and wrote about his leaving the town on the front page. He had enlarged the church both in membership and size. During his twelve years there, he had increased church attendance by 235 people and helped raise the funds to add a five-room addition, new heating plant and new Schantz organ, manufactured in Orrville, to the church. He had also been active in the community, volunteering for a number of different organizations.

The Caldwells' new home in Cleveland was on East 118th Street near Western Reserve University where Barbara had been working at the time as a secretary to six professors. Barbara actually moved in with her parents for a while.

However, by the time Chuck arrived home in 1945, Barbara had married Tom Gardner, a librarian. The couple had moved to New York where Tom headed up a research library at Columbia University. Tom hadn't been able to join the service during the war because he had heart problems that excluded him from service. Chuck did take the train to New York to visit them.

He also returned to Orrville one weekend to see his old friends who still lived there. Every boy in Chuck's class served in the military during WWII, but two of them never returned home. Both his class valedictorian and salutatorian had been killed in the fighting overseas. The salutatorian's name was Dale Arnold. He had been a friend of Chuck's, but Dale had become a pilot for the army and was shot down over the Pacific. The old friends and classmates put together a party and got drunk celebrating.

When Chuck was in his parents' home in Cleveland, he spent time reacquainting himself with his parents and exploring the new house. He didn't feel like he was home. Home had been in Orrville. This place was unknown to home, although his parents had lived here nearly three years.

He placed his Japanese rifle out of the way on the landing going to the basement. But when he went to look for it later, he saw that it wasn't his rifle but a Civil War rifle. Chuck saw seven notches carved into the stock of the rifle. It was probably to mark the number of squirrels shot, but it may have marked Yankees shot.

He asked his mother where it had come from.

"It belonged to your grandfather," she told him.

"I've never seen it before," Chuck replied. "When did it come into the family?"

His mother looked at him oddly. "Well, you used to play with it when you dressed up as a Civil War soldier."

"I've never seen it before."

"Don't you remember the sword?"

He did remember the Civil War sword. Bonnie and Bess Baker had given it to him when the Caldwells had lived in Penney Farm, Florida.

Chuck looked at the rifle again. "I have never seen that rifle."

"Well, you have seen it now."

Apparently, the new home had even scrambled some of Chuck's memories.

Chuck and his mother during his 1945 leave in Cleveland. Courtesy of Chuck Caldwell.

After a week or so with his parents, he took the train out to New York to visit a few days with his sister and her husband, whom Chuck had never met. It was a pleasant visit and they did some sightseeing.

Chuck headed back home. As the time for his leave drew to a close, he wondered if he would be sent back overseas. His mother worried about it, too.

"Is there anything that I could do to get you an extension? I hate to see you go back," she asked one evening.

Chuck shrugged. "I could get an extension if I got malaria again."

His mother leaned closer to him. "Now I don't want you to be real sick, but is there anything I could do to help you get it?"

Thinking his mother was joking, Chuck replied, "Yes, if I sit down and do some concentrated drinking, I'd probably get it."

Chuck left a short time later to walk down to Slovenia Hall where he had a couple drinks. He wasn't trying to get drunk, and indeed, by the time he walked from the hall to his parents' home, he was sober.

He walked up to his room and found a bottle of whiskey on the dresser in his room.

"The message was very clear: Drink it. So I did," Chuck said.

When Chuck woke up in the morning, he had a fever and his teeth were chattering. His malaria had returned.

1945
A WAR ENDS, A MARRIAGE BEGINS

Chuck spent the next week or so in bed sweating, shaking, and suffering through his bout of malaria. His parents drove him to the Allerton Hotel in Cleveland, which was operating as a temporary Navy hospital run by WAVES (Women Accepted for Volunteer Emergency Service). The WAVES had been formed in 1942 as the women's branch of the Naval Reserves. They served in stateside postings, which freed up sailors and officers for overseas duty in the war.

The Allerton Hotel was a sixteen-story building built in 1926. It was one of a chain of hotels in the Midwest. It had originally featured 600 apartment-style rooms with men and women living on different floors. The hotel had converted the male-only floors left vacant by men who had been drafted into the service and used them as hospital wards. There weren't many patients suffering from injuries. Primarily, it was made up of men who had served in the Pacific Theater and had returned home only to suffer a malaria attack like Chuck, although the other men probably hadn't had help from their mothers to bring on the attack.

Chuck's attack wasn't severe so he began feeling better after a day or two of bed rest. He began talking with the serviceman in the bed next to his. Sam Aydlette was a Marine who had also suffered a malaria attack. The two men became friendly during their time in the hospital as they talked about their shared experience in the war, sports, and their treatment in the hospital.

One day, two women came into the room to visit with Sam.

Sam introduced Chuck to his wife, Mary, and Mary's friend, Jacqueline Murphy, who was a petite blonde. Both of the women were WAVES who worked at the hospital.

The four of them passed a couple of enjoyable hours talking and laughing before the women had to leave. That evening, Chuck was given permission to go home the next day. He also found out that he had been given a ten-day extension on his leave. At that time, he would have to return to the hospital for blood work to see how severe his malaria was, but until that time, he could recover at home. So his mother's plan had worked. He was going to be home for a while longer.

When Chuck was checking out of the hospital, he saw a familiar face among the Navy officers doing the administrative work.

He walked up to her and said, "You're the Angel of Mercy."

The young woman smiled at him and said, "You've been to MOB4, haven't you?"

Chuck nodded. This was the nurse who had gone around MOB4 in Auckland leaving whiskey miniatures on the beds of the patients. It had brought a lot of relief to the men in the hospital and was greatly appreciated.

Chuck thanked the nurse again and told her how much her little gifts had meant to him and the other men.

He went home and climbed into bed. He may have been released but he was still feeling weak from his malaria attack. A few days later he went back to the hospital in the Allerton Hotel for a checkup.

After getting a clean bill of health, Chuck was heading home when he met Sam walking on the street. His former roommate had also been released from the hospital and had apparently been celebrating the fact by drinking his lunch.

"You should have stayed over," Sam told him. "Jackie and Mary came by and brought a whole bunch of goodies for us."

Chuck immediately wished that he had stayed in the hospital another day because had enjoyed talked with Jackie. Who wouldn't enjoy spending time with a pretty girl?

"Where can I see her?" Chuck asked. "I'd like to thank her."

Sam grinned, seeing right through Chuck's excuse. He told Chuck where Jackie worked in the Allerton and Chuck quickly excused himself.

Chuck had worn his uniform when he came in for his checkup so as he walked back into the Allerton, he acted as if he belonged there. Most of the hospital personnel saw his uniform and thought nothing of seeing him roaming the halls as he headed for the floor where Jackie worked.

He looked in open doors and scanned over the high counters, hoping to see her head. When he finally did spot her, he waved until he got her attention. Jackie got up from her desk and walked over to talk to him.

"What are you doing up here?" she asked.

"I came to thank you for all the goodies that you sent," Chuck told her.

"You're welcome, but you're not allowed up here. It's a highly restricted area." She worked in the death gratuities department.

Under a time restraint, Chuck quickly asked her out and she accepted. When he left the Allerton, he was feeling better than he had in a long while.

Chuck took Jackie to a pub for drinking for their first date. It was a popular date location for Marines and sailors. Chuck was a Marine and Jackie was part of the Navy so it seemed the natural thing to do. He felt comfortable and could work his charm on her. While he was on his leave extension, Chuck and Jackie went on three dates.

"After the first date, we didn't do any drinking," Chuck said. "We just talked."

Jackie had been raised by an aunt and uncle after her parents had died when she was a child. Her aunt, Jessie Mohler, was a Russian Jew and her uncle, Frank Mohler, was a World War I veteran of German ancestry, but they raised Jackie as a Catholic.

Yeoman Third Class Jackie Murphy. Courtesy of Chuck Caldwell.

Jackie Murphy graduated South High in Youngstown, Ohio, in 1941 and worked at the Youngstown Library until she enlisted in the WAVES in December 1943. Once in the military, she had trained at Hunter College in New York City and at Cedar Falls, Iowa. She had reported to Cleveland for duty as a Yeoman in the WAVES in June 1944.

For their third date, Chuck brought Jackie home to meet his parents. The four of them had a nice dinner while Jackie and the Caldwells got to know each other. After the dinner, Chuck's parents left for an appointment while Chuck and Jackie stayed at the house listening to music.

Chuck remembers the moment well. He was sitting in a lounge chair with Jackie sitting on his lap. They were listening to Opus No. 1 by Tommy Dorsey.

Then things got a bit confusing. "I must have said something," Chuck said. "I don't remember what it was, but the next thing I knew, we were engaged. So whatever it was, I must have said the right thing."

Chuck's leave extension ended soon thereafter and he went back on active duty. Luckily, he wasn't sent back overseas. He rode the train back to Parris Island. It wasn't so bad being there the second time. He was no longer a recruit. He was a battle-hardened Marine even if he was still a private first class. Rather than being yelled at by drill instructors, he was just left alone. For the first couple months that Chuck was there, he worked with a large group of Marines just clearing brush and cutting down weeds on the island. These were other Marines like him; men who had fought overseas and had been rotated back to the states to finish out the war. When they weren't working, they just sat around and talked and smoked.

Parris Island wasn't nearly so bad when it was seen from this perspective. He saw a lot of other boots coming in from different places in the country, and he watched the drill instructors tear them all down in order to build up a Marine. Chuck was sure glad that he was done with all that, but having been in combat, he could see why it was done. These boots were getting worked hard all the time and it would help them survive if they were shipped overseas.

When Chuck finished his brush-cutting duty, he was sent to serve with the Parris Island Fire Department. He lived on the second floor of the fire department and when the alarm would sound, he would slide down the fire pole into the bay where the equipment was stored. This was easy duty for long stretches followed by short stretches of stress as the Marines set off to fight a fire. However, these firemen were battle-hardened Marines so even that didn't create too much worry.

No. 1 Fire Department, Marine Barracks, Parris Island, S. C.

A postcard shot of the Parris Island Fire Department.

Chuck wrote Jackie often. They talked about getting married when the war ended, but their separation convinced the both of them that they didn't want to wait that long, especially since they didn't know how much longer the war would last. The Allies had achieved victory in Europe in April, but the Japanese were still fighting in the Pacific and showed no signs of letting up.

Once Jackie was discharged from the Navy Reserve, she came to Beaufort, South Carolina, the closest town to Parris Island.

Chuck and Jackie were married in the post chapel on Parris Island on August 17, 1945. It was a small ceremony since neither Chuck's parents nor Jackie's foster parents could afford to make the trip to Beaufort.

The Japanese announced their surrender on August 15, so the Caldwells did wind up waiting until after the war ended before marrying, although they didn't plan it that way.

Mr. and Mrs. Charles Caldwell on their wedding day. Courtesy of Chuck Caldwell.

The newlyweds rented a room in a mansion along the waterfront in Beaufort. They were one of five couples living in the big house. They had the bedroom in the attic, which was where the most-recent move-ins always stayed. As couples would move out, the couple living above could move down closer to the ground floor. The newlyweds didn't have to worry about cooking because part of everyone's rent went to paying for a cook.

Chuck continued working for the Parris Island Fire Department so every day he would ride the bus to the island to pull his duty.

His enlistment ended on December 29, 1945, four years after he had joined the Marines. However, when a captain handed him his discharge papers to look over, Chuck was surprised to see so many mistakes.

"This paper goes with us the rest of our lives, right?" Chuck asked.

"It sure does," the captain replied.

"Well, there's a lot of things wrong here."

"Can you prove it?"

"I sure can."

So Chuck submitted evidence to show where he had served, but it took a few days for the captain to verify everything. He was finally discharged from the Marine Corps as a corporal on January 3, 1946.

He and Jackie climbed on the first train they could catch for Cleveland. He had thirty days pay so when he got back to his parents' house, he relaxed and got reacquainted with civilian life.

When the last of his pay ran out, Chuck found himself a job with the Telling & Belle Vernon Dairy.

His job was to check all of the cases of milk bottles coming back from the trucks and put them on a conveyor belt. He also had to make sure that the cases weren't stacked too high, otherwise they wouldn't fit through the opening at the top of the conveyor belt where the cases passed into the dairy building.

"It was a terrible job, just terrible," Chuck said.

He lasted six weeks at the job before he jumped at the first thing he could find. He got the chance when he happened to meet up with a friend from the service.

"Chuck, are you happy with your dairy job?" his friend asked.

That was an easy question to answer. "No," Chuck told him.

"I think I've got one you might be interested in working for the War Department." Sensing Chuck might protest, he rushed on quickly. "You don't have to go back into the service to do it."

The job was at the Cleveland Post Office on Superior Avenue in downtown Cleveland. The five-story Beaux-Arts building had a large receiving area set aside for inspecting military packages. Chuck's new job entailed, inspecting military footlockers that were being shipped stateside by servicemen.

A serviceman from each of the military branches was hired to work in the inspection room. Chuck was the Marine representative. He worked with a soldier from the 101st Airborne, a sailor, and even an airman from the U. S. Army Air Forces, the predecessor to the U.S. Air Force. They had all fought the war in different areas.

"The 101st guy was never sober a minute," Chuck said. "He came in drunk and he stayed drunk. He just slept over in the corner."

They would run the footlockers through a precursor to an x-ray machine to see if weapons or other contraband were being shipped home. Because this was an early version of the x-ray machine, Chuck and the other servicemen didn't know enough to protect themselves from the radiation leaking from it.

"Many of these boxes came from France and they had all kinds of wine in them," Chuck said. "We would take the wine out, check the tag to see where the box was being shipped and let the recipient know he had a package."

Unlike weapons that were found, the recipient could still get the wine if he paid the taxes on it.

To keep things on the up and up, FBI agents watched the floor and the inspectors from windows high up near the ceiling.

One box came in from a lieutenant colonel. It didn't have a bill of lading on the outside like it was supposed to so it had to be opened and inspected.

"It must have had a thousand Mylflam cigarette lighters in it that had come from a PX," Chuck said.

Chuck and Jackie Caldwell. Courtesy of Chuck Caldwell.

The colonel was told he had a package waiting for him and when he came to retrieve it, the FBI agents were waiting for him instead.

Chuck decided that he wanted to pursue his college degree

so he could get a job he enjoyed rather than something to just pay the bills. Despite his earlier failure as a student, Chuck had matured and was ready to learn and there was only one place he wanted to go for that and it was the University of Alabama.

Using the G. I. Bill, it wouldn't cost him anything to attend college, but being married, he couldn't stay at the same dorm he had stayed in 1941. Chuck thought that he had made arrangements for this. He had known that he wanted to return to college since 1944. He had even written to the University of Alabama to ask that his name be put on the housing waiting list. He didn't know exactly when he would be returning to the university, but he knew that the waiting list for campus housing was long, very long. Henry Siker, assistant to the Dean of Students, wrote him back and said that Chuck's name was added to the list.

When Chuck and Jackie arrived in Tuscaloosa, he checked in with the campus housing office to see where they would be living. He was told that his name wasn't even on the list. Chuck couldn't believe it. He pulled out the letter saying that his name had been added to the list.

Sikir was called in. He looked at the letter and said, "We'll put you on the list right now."

"How about you put me on the list when you wrote me the letter?" Chuck told him. "That's a lot of names on there before mine."

Dean Siker said that he couldn't move Chuck ahead on the list. He could only add Chuck's name to the end of the existing list. Chuck told him where he could stick that list using the colorful language the Marines had taught him.

He and Jackie never did live on campus. Their first place was a rented room in a farmhouse outside of town where they also had kitchen privileges. Then they heard about a war hospital that the university had acquired and converted into housing for married veterans. It was located off campus. Chuck and

Jackie rented an apartment in the Northington and ate meals in the cafeteria.

Since the apartments weren't on campus, Chuck had to walk a mile down a gravel road to catch a bus to take him to his classes on campus.

In order to avoid the problems he had had as a freshman in 1941, Chuck put together a plan for taking his classes. "I figured if I took the subjects that I didn't like, but I had to take first and get them over with – things like biology, foreign languages, etc. – by the time I was a junior, I would have all of the required courses over with and I would be able to just take art classes," Chuck said.

Although he still loved the Crimson Tide, he had learned his lesson about working as part of the team. It wasn't for him anymore, especially since he was now a married man with a young wife who wanted his attention. He could only be split so many ways.

He did join a fraternity, though, only it wasn't the one that he had pledged in 1941.

"I was pledged to Delta Chi, but after the war, I decided that I didn't want to deal with childish hazing," Chuck said.

Instead, he joined Alpha Sigma Omega, an honorary arts fraternity. It had been only a campus club until it received its charter from Alpha Sigma Omega in 1946. In 1947, Chuck was one of seven members, both male and female, who met to learn more about art and to practice their skills.

One advantage of living at Northington was that it had a pool. The university didn't have one at the time. If students wanted to swim, they swam in a lake on campus. Chuck got a part-time job as a life guard at the pool to earn spending money for him and Jackie.

Jackie was taking some classes herself on the G. I. Bill. Her classes were for a home-economics degree. She became pregnant in 1947 and she and Chuck were delighted to be starting their new family. They started making plans to move to a larger apartment and buying baby clothes and diapers. Then Jackie miscarried in December, which put a damper on their Christmas.

After Jackie lost the baby, she filled some of her hours working at a local paper mill, which Chuck said sent an "unflushed toilet smell all over the campus."

They lived a simple life, but they had barely been married a year so they were still enjoying spending time with each other. It was all they needed.

Chuck's sculpting skills happened to get him in the newspaper again during the winter of 1948. It was an odd winter for Tuscaloosa because the city typically has temperatures in the upper fifties in the winter. During the beginning of 1948, Tuscaloosa had snow twice. The second snowfall in February was even enough to make snowballs for a snowball fight or snowmen.

Chuck had made friends with a couple other guys from Ohio who lived in Northington with their wives. When the snow stopped, they went out and made a snow woman who had all her curves in the right places. The *Tuscaloosa News* photographer came out and snapped a photo that ran the next day in the newspaper.

As he continued to work and attend classes, Chuck found a job working for Dr. David DeJarnette who was studying the Moundville Indian site in Tuscaloosa. For 450 years beginning in 1000 A.D., the site had been occupied by the Mississippian culture. A village was built overlooking the Black Warrior River. DeJarnette had conducted the first large-scale excavation of the site in 1929.

Unlike typical Indian villages, the Moundville site was 300 acres, much of which was surrounded by a wooden palisade. In the central plaza of the city are twenty-six earthen mounds with buildings on them. Some of the buildings were homes of the city nobles. Others had other purposes, such as a mortuary.

Why this particular form of architecture was used is not known, but it does resemble flattened pyramids that can be found in Central America. Although those pyramids are made from stone not earth.

Chuck and a friend working on their full-figured snow woman that appeared in the *Tuscaloosa News*. Courtesy of Chuck Caldwell.

Moundville was a true city. It was not a farming village. The farmers lived outside of the city and paid a tribute to the city, essentially a tax. It was this tribute that supported the city residents.

Around 1350 A.D. the city seems to have become more ceremonial and religious than a proper city. By the time the Europeans arrived in the 1540s, it was abandoned. How the

Mississippian Culture is related to the typical Native American tribes is not understood and still being studied.

Dr. DeJarnette started a museum at the university about Moundville. When he needed a sculptor to make his displays, Chuck jumped at the chance to work as an artist. He primarily made a lot of prehistoric animals to fill the displays that showed Moundville at different periods of its history.

As the summer of 1949 approached, Chuck was a senior and close to graduating. He had 290 credit hours and needed ten more to graduate. He had completed and passed all of his required subjects with ease unlike his first freshman semester in 1941.

He was going to be able to finish his coursework during the summer with two final classes: typography and U.S. Naval History. He expected to be able to graduate at the end of August.

Then Dr. DeJarnette left the university to move to Oak Ridge, Tennessee, and run the newly established American Museum of Atomic Energy.

As Chuck's last semester started, DeJarnette called him and asked, "How soon can you get out here?"

DeJarnette had been so impressed by Chuck's work for the Moundville Archaeological Museum that he wanted him to work in the new museum designing and building displays telling the story of nuclear energy and the atomic bomb.

"The quarter is over at the end of August," Chuck told him.

"I want you out here by the twenty-third of July and up at Oak Ridge, Tennessee," DeJarnette told him. "I've got a job for you to do."

The museum had opened in an old cafeteria from the days when the facility had been in active use as part of the atomic bomb project. DeJarnette wanted to have visitors taken on a guided tour that showed them how atomic energy could benefit mankind.

"I'll have to talk to the dean," Chuck said.

"Then do that and get back to me."

Chuck was in classes from 8 a.m. to 5 p.m. and then he worked until 9 p.m. He wasn't sure when he would be able to talk with the dean, but he wasn't going to pass up this opportunity. He talked it over with Jackie who was supportive of the idea.

The dean told Chuck he needed to finish his current two courses and he would get his degree. In order to do that and be in Oak Ridge by July 23, he would have to take the courses in an accelerated manner, cramming the same amount of material into half of the time. The lead typography course was no problem. Chuck already had a strong A and the teacher was willing to pass him. The naval history course was taught by a former professor at the U. S. Naval Academy.

"He knew I was headed for a job so he said, 'I'm going to give you two questions. You can take your pick,'" Chuck said.

One of the topics was German submarines in World War I or U.S. Naval operations during World War II. It was an easy choice for Chuck.

Typically, an essay question answer doesn't fill a small blue exam book, but Chuck filled three of them answering the question on his final exam.

He had passed his last two classes with As and was a graduate of the University of Alabama, although he never got to wear a cap and gown and attend his graduation ceremony. Chuck and Jackie packed up their belongings and arrived in Oak Ridge on July 23.

1949–1958
MUSHROOM CLOUDS

The 1941 Ford station wagon with wooden sides was packed with everything that Jackie and Chuck owned, which wasn't even enough to fill the vehicle. They had lived in a furnished apartment in Tuscaloosa so most everything stayed behind except for clothing, some blankets, boxes of school books, and of course Chuck's art supplies. The only furniture that came with them was a single wooden chair.

Oak Ridge, Tennessee, was an unusual city, which was quite obvious when Chuck drove past an old guard post as he entered the city. The booth was unmanned, but that hadn't always been the case. In fact, the guard booths had been manned until a few months earlier. Not only were the shotgun-wielding guards missing but so were large sections of the fence that had surrounded the city.

For years, Oak Ridge had been a hidden city, one of three places in the country where the atomic bomb had been developed (the other two being Los Alamos, New Mexico, and Hanford, Washington). It had been so secret that even misleading names were given the site. It was originally called Kingston Demolition Range, after nearby Kingston, Tennessee. The name had frightened area residents, though, and it had been changed to the more-innocuous-sounding Clinton Engineer Works.

Oak Ridge was originally a 59,000-acre military encampment that sprang up from nowhere in 1942 when the federal government took over farms and small communities in the mountains of Tennessee. The creation of the new city wiped out five small communities in the area, in much the same way many of the New Deal public works projects had driven people from their homes and farms when the government decided it needed the land. In fact, some of the families displaced to build Clinton Engineer Works had been displaced twice before when the government created the Smokey Mountains National Park and the Norris Dam.

The new community was created inside miles of barbed wire. It was a restricted community where a resident's pass was needed to enter at one of the seven gates and lie-detector tests were common. Speaking about your work was discouraged and the employees were given only the barest minimum amount of information needed to do their jobs.

"Oak Ridge in those years contained no jails, no courts, no funeral homes, and no cemeteries. Any births or deaths would be recorded as having occurred in nearby town, so as not to give hints about the size of the population. To further protect anonymity, even high school athletes' last names were absent from the backs of their jerseys," Lindsey A. Freeman wrote in *Longing for the Bomb.*

It was only after the first atomic bomb was dropped on Hiroshima that most Oak Ridgers realized what they had been doing in the mountains of Tennessee. Oak Ridge scientists created the first large-scale plutonium reactor and then they worked at separating isotopes of uranium-238 to create uranium-235, a fissionable material. The labs at Oak Ridge produced the fissionable material used in the first atomic bomb called Little Boy that was dropped on Hiroshima.

After the war, when everyone knew about the atomic bomb, there was still a need for security about the sites where plutonium was created, but not at the level that it had been at during the war. Control of Oak Ridge was given over to the newly created Atomic Energy Commission and the town opened up somewhat. The X-10 plant became the Oak Ridge National Laboratory and focused on the peaceful uses of atomic energy while the town's other two plants Y-12 and

K-25 continued to produce uranium-235 for the nation's atomic stockpile.

Although work still needed to be done in those plants dealing with atomic energy, the same number of employees weren't needed to accomplish it. Population in Oak Ridge dropped from its peak of 75,000 during the war to 43,000 in June 1946. Some of the poorly-constructed residential areas became ghost towns.

"If you wander through the woods and you know where to look, you can find lonely fire hydrants and evidence of pathways that worked as streets of the former community," Freeman wrote.

Soon after the war ended, a debate raged in Congress over whether the military should maintain control over Oak Ridge and the technology housed within its borders. Some thought the secrets of atomic energy were too dangerous to risk being discovered by enemies of the United States. Others believed atomic energy had many peaceful purposes that should be shared with mankind. In the end, the latter argument won, and the Atomic Energy Commission was created.

The commission managed the city after the war, but the goal was to eventually turn Oak Ridge into a public city. For this to happen, the land, which was federally owned, had to become private property so that the property owners could request incorporation.

One step towards independence for Oak Ridge was the opening of the gates at the entrances to the city. This was not a popular decision. A straw poll of residents at a town meeting had 157 voting against opening the gates and only seventeen voting for it. Residents feared that crime would increase. The move to opening up Oak Ridge would also mean a large reduction in the amount of tax dollars pouring into the town that led to a number of services and amenities not typically available in a town its size.

"Oak Ridgers did not pay taxes, were given free coal, and enjoyed free or very inexpensive medical care and incredibly cheap rents, and all maintenance services were provided free of charge," Freeman wrote.

The opening of the gates of Oak Ridge happened on March 19, 1949, four and a half months before Chuck and Jackie would arrive. It was a large media event that featured a miniature bomb explosion.

"A standard ribbon-cutting ceremony executed with a snip of scissor blades would have been far too gauche for this science city of the future. In its place, a mini-simulacrum of an atomic bomb blast was ignited, setting ablaze the scarlet ribbon that stretched across the city's main gate," Freeman wrote.

An estimated 10,000 people attended along with U.S. government officials and Hollywood celebrities. Besides the opening ceremony, the gate-opening celebration featured a parade, fashion show, banquet and dance. Singer and actress Marie "The Body" McDonald was crowned "Miss Atomic Blonde."

Lost among all of the hoopla of the gate opening was the opening of the world's first museum dedicated to atomic energy in the former cafeteria where workers had once spent their lunch hours. The American Museum of Atomic Energy had first started as a traveling exhibition, sponsored by the Atomic Energy Commission. It sought to feature all of the positive aspects of atomic energy. It drew over one million visitors in June 1948 at the Golden Jubilee Celebration in New York City. The Oak Ridge museum featured displays of atomic energy's uses in medicine, agriculture, peace, and energy.

Once the decision was made to give it a permanent home, David DeJarnette was appointed as the curator. He said the mission of the museum was "to tell the story of atomic energy in such a way that it will be interesting and understandable to young and old."

Admission to the museum was twenty-five cents with children under twelve paying only five cents. The money was used to run the museum and create new exhibits.

Chuck and Jackie's first home in Oak Ridge was a one-bedroom apartment on Vermont Avenue, a circular residential street next to the hospital and just a few blocks from the Oak Ridge downtown area. The city was still filled with more businesses than would typically be found in a city the size of Oak Ridge, including four bowling alleys, ten clothing stores, sixteen dentists, and twenty-two grocery stores. During the war, all of these stores had been overcrowded with customers who waited in long lines to purchase their merchandise or services. With the end of the war and the shrinking of the population, the lines had disappeared.

Although Oak Ridge boasted sixteen restaurants, Chuck and Jackie quickly learned that if they wanted to eat out, it was better to drive the twenty miles into Knoxville. Oak Ridge had been built quickly in the 1940s and because of this, large areas had been clear cut of trees to make room for new, quickly constructed houses and buildings. This led to a mud problem in the city that was only partially solved by building boardwalks along the streets and in front of businesses. It helped keep people out of the mud, but the boardwalk couldn't reach everywhere and where they couldn't reach, there was mud, lots of mud. Many of the local businesses raised their prices on wet days when customers tracked pounds of mud across the floors of their businesses. Prices were still being raised in 1949, even though trees and shrubbery had been planted to help deal with the mud problem.

At first, Chuck enjoyed his work at the museum under Dr. DeJarnette. He attended classes to learn the basics of atomic energy. He then used that knowledge to create engaging displays of how reactors worked, a model of a particle accelerator, and maps that showed the extent of the damage in Hiroshima and Nagasaki from the bombs detonated there to end WWII. He created a display that took visitors from the mining of uranium through the production of isotopes to the lighting of a city.

His displays were even featured on the front of an Esso map for the state of Tennessee.

One of the many displays, models, and maps that Chuck made for the American Museum of Atomic Energy. Courtesy of Chuck Caldwell.

Besides Chuck's models, drawings and miniatures, other exhibits included a Van de Graaf generator that used a moving belt to create a moving electrical spark around a metal globe or a Geiger counter for detecting radioactive charges. A popular exhibit allowed visitors to have a dime placed in a machine and irradiated. It was a low-level charge that soon dissipated, but for the time it could trigger the clicks of a Geiger counter, visitors were delighted. Irradiated dimes could also be purchased in the gift shop along with small pieces of uranium.

Freeman wrote of an unusual exhibit in the museum called "Radioactive Turtles." Children could use a sliding Geiger counter to detect the radioactive shells of turtles as they meandered among their non-radioactive counterparts.

Dr. DeJarnette soon left the museum to head back to the University of Alabama and the new museum director had no qualms about pulling his designers away from their work to be tour guides. All too often the work that Chuck loved doing was interrupted with calls from the main museum floor to Chuck's basement office. The museum director would want Chuck to take a group of school kids on a tour of the museum because the museum was so busy that extra help was needed. People wanted to know about atomic energy. They had seen its destructive force in movies and pictures and had heard the stories of the dangers of radiation. The 20,000 visitors to the museum in 1949 wanted to know more.

Chuck would have to take off his apron and wash the clay and paint from his hands to go upstairs to lead the tour. He knew the basics of how atomic energy worked, but he didn't consider himself qualified to answer the questions from the tourists. He also didn't like doing it because it put him behind in the work that he enjoyed doing.

On June 25, 1950, the Korean People's Army in North Korea crossed the thirty-eighth parallel into South Korea. The escalation of the tensions between North and South Korea started a war that America and other United Nations countries were soon drawn into.

Chuck was surprised to find himself called back to active duty. While at the University of Alabama in December 1947, he had been convinced to join the Inactive Marine Corps Reserves for four years. He didn't have to go to boot camp again or attend any active duty training, but, of course, he didn't get any extra pay. What it did do was put him on the hook for being recalled to duty, which was done when war broke out in Korea.

Luckily, he didn't have to go overseas to fight. Chuck was sent to Camp Lejeune in North Carolina to help train new Marines. For the most part, his work was routine and boring. He found himself with a lot of time on his hands, so much so, that he illustrated his Guadalcanal diary, drawing a single panel for each day in the journal.

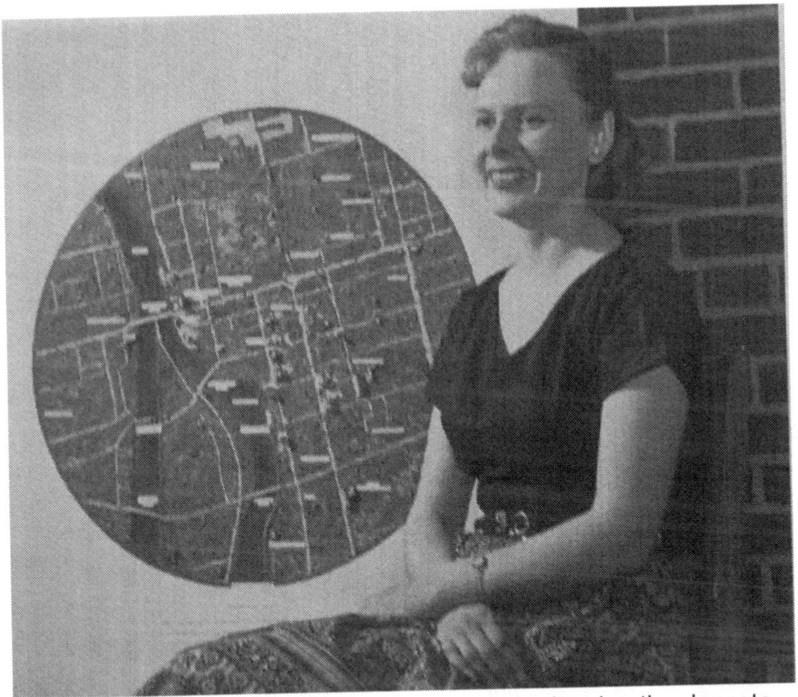

Jackie Caldwell in front of a map Chuck made showing the devastation of the Hiroshima atomic bomb explosion for the American Museum of Atomic Energy. Courtesy of Chuck Caldwell.

Jackie had a secretarial job with the Atomic Energy Commission so she stayed in Oak Ridge. Chuck and other Marines in the area commuted back to Tennessee every weekend to see their families that had remained behind.

"Each weekend, we would get a fifty-mile-radius pass, but

me and the other guys from Oak Ridge, Knoxville, and East Tennessee would drive the 300 miles to Oak Ridge," Chuck said.

This turned out to be more dangerous than his service during the Korean War. One time, Chuck was driving up a two-lane mountain road where "you could look off to the right and see the tops of the pine trees just below the railing." That didn't worry him as much as the two sets of headlights side by side coming down the road toward his car.

One driver's brakes had apparently failed and he couldn't slow his descent so he was trying to pass the truck in front of him. The car managed to just barely slide between Chuck's car and the truck.

"We got to the bottom of the hill and I stopped to see how close that car had come to me," Chuck said. "It had taken the paint off the side of my car."

He did this for a year until he was discharged in December 1951 as a sergeant.

When he returned to Oak Ridge, Chuck's job at the Museum of Atomic Energy was still waiting for him. He decided that some things needed to change, though.

Chuck went into his boss and said, "It's been two years now. I expect a raise and I don't want to have to give any more tours. I'm an artist not a lecturer."

His boss told him that he couldn't agree to that so Chuck quit. He took a job as an engineering draftsman drawing charts for the Graphic Arts Department of the Oak Ridge National Laboratory Information Division. He quickly found out that it was "the most boring work in the world", but at least it paid more than he had been making.

When he returned home, he also got some disturbing news. His parents, who had been married for thirty-three years had gotten divorced while he was at Camp Lejeune and his mother had gotten married again.

"It was quite a shock," Chuck said. "I never did find out why and I never did ask."

The Caldwells' Cemesto house at 110 South Tampa Lane in Oak Ridge. Courtesy of Chuck Caldwell.

Early in 1954, Jackie told Chuck that she was pregnant. It had been seven years since she had been pregnant and lost their first child. Their one-bedroom apartment on Vermont Lane was going to be too small for a family, but at least it was within walking distance of the hospital. Chuck put in for larger housing, which they were eligible for since Jackie was pregnant.

Shortly before Jackie delivered her baby, the Caldwells moved to a small house on South Tampa Lane. It was a one-story, two-bedroom house on a cul-de-sac. The house was made of a material called Cemesto, a combination of cement and asbestos. The homes had been quickly assembled when Oak Ridge was created during WWII. The pre-fabricated pieces were trucked to the location of the home and assembled on the foundation. The result was a home with seams along the walls inside the house where the pieces were joined.

It was the smallest house on the street, but the Caldwells eventually built a porch and full basement in 1961. The basement added two bedrooms and a fallout shelter to the house.

The Caldwells enjoyed the neighborhood. Plenty of other families on the street had young children. The families often got together to hold neighborhood parties and the children played together.

The problem was not only was Chuck two miles further away from work, Jackie was also further away from the hospital. He prayed that his wife would give him plenty of warning so he could get her to the hospital in time.

Chuck Caldwell and his son, David. Courtesy of Chuck Caldwell.

In November, Jackie delivered a healthy baby boy whom his parents named David.

With another member of the family, Chuck was locked into his job, no matter how boring it became.

Chuck's interest in history continued as did his interest in art.

He started attending re-enactments of Civil War battles in 1956. One of those re-enactments was the Battle of Spotsylvania. When Chuck arrived on the battlefield, he was spooked.

"On glancing around, I got an eerie feeling that I had been there before," Chuck said. "Everywhere I looked, familiar landscapes greeted me although I had never set foot there. My memory told me that if I should look over my shoulder to the west, a huge tree would be there. I slowly turned, and there it was—an unforgettable gnarled oak just as I had imagined it."

It wasn't until years later when he was looking through some of his old papers that he came across a roster of the original participants at the Battle of Spotsylvania and realized that he had known one of the men. Chuck had sat at his feet as a young boy and listened to his stories of the battle over and over again until it must have become part of his memory.

Many of those old veterans whom Chuck had met in 1938 had died after the Gettysburg reunion and the few that remained were quickly dying.

A number of men claimed to be the last living Confederate veteran. These men died throughout the 1950's. Many of their claims were debunked as more information about their births was uncovered. The largest problem in verifying their claims was that many Confederate records had been destroyed or lost because the Confederate government had no official archive system.

John B. Salling was one of those men with a questionable provenance. He claimed to have been born in 1846 and fought for the Confederate Army during the Civil War.

Chuck found out that Salling was living in Slant, Virginia. He drove there after the Battle of Spotsylvania re-enactment in

1956 with David who was only two years old. They found the aged veteran living in a little wooden frame house. Salling was among the soldiers whom Chuck had met in 1938 at Gettysburg.

The veterans from two different wars talked for a while and Salling put on his uniform with all its reunion ribbons.

"He couldn't hear very well, but he was a talker," Chuck said.

Before he left, Chuck made sure to get a picture of him, David and Salling.

Salling died in 1959 and was believed to have been the second-to-the-last veteran of the Civil War. Walter Williams of Texas was believed for a time to have been the last surviving veteran of the Civil War. However, census research over the years found that both of those men's claims were in error and they did not even serve in the Civil War.

The last Confederate veteran, whose service could be authenticated, was Pleasant Crump who was 104 years old when he died on December 31, 1951.

Crump was an Alabamian. Near the end of the Civil War, he and a friend traveled to Petersburg, Virginia, and they enlisted in the Tenth Alabama Infantry in November 1864. He saw action during the war and was also present at General Robert E. Lee's surrender at Appomattox Court House.

However, the last Union veteran and the last Civil War veteran was Albert Woolson, who died in 1956 at the age of 109. He had been born in 1847 in Antwerp, New York.

Albert's father had enlisted in the Union Army and was wounded in the Battle of Shiloh. His wounds were treated at an army hospital in Windom, Minnesota, but he eventually died. Not before Albert and his mother had moved there to be close to him.

After Albert's father died, Albert joined the First Minnesota Heavy Artillery Regiment as a drummer boy on August 10, 1864. He never saw any action and was discharged on September 7, 1865.

He died of lung congestion in Duluth, Minnesota, on August 2, 1956, and was buried with full military honors at Park Hill Cemetery.

President Dwight D. Eisenhower said, following Woolson's death, "The American people have lost the last personal link with the Union Army ... His passing brings sorrow to the hearts of all of us who cherished the memory of the brave men on both sides of the War Between the States."

Chuck's own bravery during World War II was recognized the following year when he was awarded a Purple Heart for the wounds he had received on Guadalcanal fifteen years earlier.

That same year, Chuck finally got a break in his work monotony. One of the higher ups at institute came to the graphic arts department looking for volunteers.

"We're looking for someone who can withstand the heat," the man said.

Chuck thought that since he had fought in the Pacific during WWII, he could certainly withstand the heat.

Then the official said, "We're looking for someone who can stand living with a group of men for a long time."

Chuck also thought that he fit the bill. After all, he had also done just that in WWII. So he volunteered and got the assignment to spend the summer out at the Nevada Atomic Test Site.

In 1948, before Chuck had even arrived in Oak Ridge, the U. S. government had selected a site in the Great Basin in Nevada to serve as the primary nuclear testing site in the United States. It wasn't until January 1951 that the actual testing of atomic bombs started, though.

The Nevada Test Site was part of a group of sites in the state used for nuclear testing. Other sites included the Nellis Air Force Range near Las Vegas, the Central Nevada Test Area near Eureka, and the Project Shoal Site near Fallon. The Nevada sites were part of fifteen nuclear testing sites that would be used over forty-seven years of nuclear testing in the United States. Over that time "bombs would be dropped from planes, detonated atop metal towers, exploded from anchored balloons and barges, and fired underground and underwater."

Although the scientists developing nuclear bombs knew about fallout, it wasn't until the bombs were actually detonated that it could be measured and then it was discovered that the fallout range had been underestimated in many cases.

Michon Mackedon wrote in *Bombast*, "In the end, however, the site nomination relied on unproven hypotheses about engineering sites and 'safe' fallout zones, and revealed geopolitical and aesthetic biases." By then, it was too late. Crops, livestock, soil, water, and even people have become unexpected victims of radiation.

Testing continued regularly with dozens of explosions each year on average.

Gladwin Hill captured the wonder and awe of those early detonations in the *New York Times*. "Then suddenly the surrounding mountains and sky were brilliantly illuminated for a fraction of a second by a strange light that seemed almost mystical.

"It was strange because, unlike light from the sun, it did not appear to have come from any source but to come from everywhere. It flashed almost too quickly to see. Yet the image that persisted for a fraction of a second afterward in the eye was unforgettable.

"It was a gray-green light of infinite coldness, apparently completely devoid of any red tones. In its momentary glare, the mountains looked in the silence like the weird and lifeless peaks of a dead planet."

However, as detonation after detonation continued, reporters and the public seemed to lose that sense of wonder. It was almost as if it was a commonplace occurrence to have a nuclear detonation nearby. "As testing became more routine, cavalier reporters described the weapon as if it were a new toy, showing off a kind of atomic connoisseurship. Atomic clouds that varied from the mushroom norm were assigned metaphorical shapes," Mackedon wrote.

Chuck preparing the fission foil balls before an atomic detonation in Nevada. Courtesy of Chuck Caldwell.

The Caldwells arrived in Nevada and were startled by the heat and sand. Even Chuck, who had fought in the tropical Pacific, was surprised. Nevada was nearly all desert and the heat was dry whereas the Pacific had been humid.

"I was really excited to be there," Chuck said. "I wanted to see what this thing was all about."

He had seen the newsreel footage of the Japanese atomic bomb detonations. You couldn't live in Oak Ridge and have not seen it multiple times. He even understood in his mind the scope of the devastation. He had even drawn maps and built models at the Museum of Atomic Energy to illustrate how devastated Hiroshima had been after the first atomic bomb explosion. Still, it was such a powerful detonation and the destruction was so vast that he just couldn't imagine seeing something that hadn't been shrunk by map scale or movie camera.

The Caldwells found a place to live near the testing site, but supposedly at a far enough distance away to not be in danger of nuclear fallout. They rented a house in Las Vegas. It was a nice house, but it had no air conditioning. Instead, it was cooled by water running through tubes on the flat roof of the house.

Chuck met with the men he would be working with and had his job explained to him. Most of the group were scientists with Ph.D.'s who were studying the effects of nuclear explosions on different fissionable materials.

One of the men was Wendell Ogg, who had served on the first organized expedition to find Noah's Ark in 1949. Ogg was also from Oak Ridge, so when he was discovered to be part of the expedition to Turkey, rumors started that the group was looking for uranium. The Soviets thought the group were spies sent to investigate Soviet nuclear activities.

Chuck's job was to help set up fissionable materials at the detonation sites for a series of explosions called Operation Plumbbob. After a bomb detonated, his team would go in after the explosion to try and find the balls of fissionable material, if they still existed.

Many of the detonation sites were amid false towns made of lightweight wood and rice paper.

"We had to have the exact same type of houses that they had in Hiroshima and Nagasaki, but there was no furniture, just walls and paper windows," Chuck said.

Once the towns were constructed, wafer-size pieces of fissionable material were placed in steel balls attached to a chain. Each chain had five or six balls so that when the chain was hung from one end, the balls were at different heights.

"Then we hauled ass in a four-door Dodge truck to get ten miles away before the bomb detonated," Chuck said.

After the bomb was dropped or detonated, Chuck's team would head back to ground zero to try and find as many of the balls of fissionable material as they could. They would record where the balls were found and how much radiation was detected. The balls were designed to simulate human organs. The point was to see what effect radiation would have on the organs at different distances.

However, while they were trying to determine the damage radiation had on human organs, they also had to make sure that they didn't damage their own. They wore radiation suits while at ground zero and radiation badges that indicated whether they were exposing themselves to too much radiation.

Chuck was excited to see his first detonation of an atomic bomb. He was all set for what he expected to be an ear-shattering explosion.

"It wasn't that noisy, but what happened afterwards is that this doughnut rolled out from the center and knocked you on your ass if you weren't kneeling down," Chuck said.

The doughnut was the concussive force of the explosion stirring up sand as it moved outward from ground zero.

One time, a photographer wanted to see what it was like to be up close to a nuclear explosion so he got permission to walk down from News Nob to where Chuck's team waited by their truck. It was about 100 yards closer to the explosion.

As the men waited for the detonation of the bomb, they rolled the windows down in their vehicle so that the windshields wouldn't shatter from the concussive force of the explosion, which could still be felt even though they were nine miles away.

The bomb went off and Chuck saw the doughnut speeding toward him.

As the doughnut grew closer, Chuck and the other men on his team kneeled on the ground and put their heads down. No one told the photographer to do so. He was too busy taking pictures.

When the concussive force hit the group, the kneeling men were buffeted back and forth a bit, but the photographer was sent tumbling head over heels and wound up laying on his back.

Chuck in his radiation protection suit before a test detonation. Courtesy of Chuck Caldwell.

"Depending on what was required, I have gone down to sites when the column was still going up," Chuck said. "Contaminated earth was going up in the air, and then it would be raining down on me."

The Nevada Test Site detonated thirty-one atomic bombs in 1957. Nearly all of them were part of Operation Plumbbob, which is the program on which Chuck worked. The yields on the bombs varied from a half ton to seventy-four kilotons. Chuck and other workers on the project collected information for improved weapon design, biomedical research, safety testing, and component and design testing for thermonuclear weapons. It was the longest and most-comprehensive test series of nuclear weapons conducted in the continental United States. It later became controversial when the amount of radiation released into the atmosphere was discovered.

The Hood Test was the largest atmospheric test ever conducted at the Nevada Test Site. It was a two-stage thermonuclear detonation, even though the government denied that thermonuclear weapons were being detonated in Nevada. The detonation took place on July 5 and Chuck was on the retrieval team. The bomb was dropped from a balloon 1,500 feet in the air.

For this one detonation, Chuck was going to have to make three recoveries. This was going to be difficult with all of the smoke and debris that would be in the area, plus it was difficult to see much in the radiation suits. He also wanted to spend as little time as possible in the area.

"The suits didn't stop the radiation," Chuck said. "It just reduced our exposure some. We had to watch our radiation tags to make sure we didn't get too much radiation."

After each detonation, doctors recorded how much radiation each person had received. If the reading was too high, then that person would have to sit out several explosions until the doctors deemed it safe for him to participate again.

Chuck laid out a path made of flat stones since they wouldn't be moved by the blast. They were stuck in the ground and offered no resistance to the blast. He set the path to take him to the fission balls set at 2,200 yards, 2,100 yards, and 2,000 yards from ground zero.

The mushroom cloud from the Hood test detonation in 1957. Courtesy of Chuck Caldwell.

Once everything was set out, Chuck and his team drove off to a safe distance. He put on his radiation suit and waited for the detonation. After the blinding flash of light faded and the concussion wave passed, he and the others drove toward ground zero.

Chuck approached ground zero in his truck, but then he had to climb up over a hill. As he topped the hill, he saw the mushroom cloud still rising into the sky and the small town that had been on the desert floor was just small bits of debris.

Chuck got out of the truck and started to walk along the path he had laid out. Even when it was difficult to see the stones, he could feel their smoothness under his feet and knew that he was on the right path. He certainly couldn't have judged it by his surroundings since nothing upright remained and fires were burning all around him.

"The fires I expected," Chuck said. "What I didn't expect was the slithering sound that I kept hearing. I thought it was the sage burning."

He couldn't hear clearly inside the suit with his breathing equipment turned on. He finally stopped and looked around for the source of the sound.

"The ground was moving!" Chuck said. "But then I realized that it wasn't the ground but thousands of lizards that lived on the mountain. They had been baked and were blind. They were running all over the place, running over my shoes, and dying!"

Despite this evidence and the radiation tags, Chuck wasn't too concerned about the radiation. He trusted the doctors to tell him when he had too much, not realizing that they were exploring new territory as well.

Chuck didn't participate on the retrieval team for all of the explosions that summer. Some he just witnessed. During one, he even brought three-year-old David into the bunker to watch. The bunker was closer to the explosions than even Chuck's team got. Most people stayed even further away at News Nob. This was where the media could come to witness the explosions.

Chuck knew that what was happening in Nevada was highly unusual and he wanted his son to be able to say that he had seen a nuclear explosion. However, David being a three-year old did not want to put on the black goggles that would protect his eyes from the blinding light of the explosion. As the countdown commenced, David kept pulling off his glasses and not listening to his father to leave them in place.

"He wouldn't put on his goggles so I had to press his face into my chest so that he was turned away from the blast," Chuck said.

Chuck's time in Nevada was not all work. He had weekends off and sometime during the week. He would spend time with his family and they would drive off to go site seeing.

During one of the trips, a group of ten people at the Nevada Test Site drove to Anaheim, California, to visit Disneyland, which had opened in 1955. Walt Disney, who had made his fortune with children's cartoons and then family-friendly films, had a vision of what he wanted an amusement park to be. He began planning what he called "Mickey Mouse Park" in 1948. The idea grew from a small eight-acre park to more than 160 acres. The park had cost $17 million to build (around $150 million in 2015 dollars).

When it opened to the public in 1955, it featured twenty attractions in the now-familiar areas of Frontierland, Tommorowland, Adventureland and Fantasyland. Opening day certainly didn't go as well as it could have and the park got a lot of bad publicity. It soon got things on the right track and the park's popularity has continued to grow since its opening.

The Caldwells enjoyed their time there immensely as did David as he rode the rides. At one point, Chuck, Jackie, and David were walking down the Main Street of the park. Chuck was surprised that it wasn't more crowded, but he wasn't complaining. Then he noticed a familiar face standing off to the side.

He leaned over and said to Jackie, "I think that's Walt Disney in front of us."

Jackie couldn't be sure so they moved off to the side to get a better look at his face. They both agreed that it was the man himself and approached him.

"Mr. Disney, could we have your autograph?" Chuck asked him.

Disney shook his head. "I'm sorry. I can't. It would draw a crowd."

The three of them spoke for a time. Disney told the Caldwells that he had a grandson about David's age. Chuck and Jackie told him that they had driven in from Nevada to visit the park and were enjoying it immensely. Disney smiled at that and told them that he kept an apartment above the shops where he could stay and watch people visiting the park.

As the Caldwells said goodbye and prepared to move off, Disney reached into his jacket pocket and pulled out a piece of paper. He handed it to them. It had his signature on it with a small sketch of Mickey Mouse.

"Enjoy your time here," he said.

The Caldwells headed back to Oak Ridge in the fall once the detonations for Operation Plumbbob ended. Chuck had to go back to doing office work and drawings once again for another few months at least.

Near the end of 1957, Jackie went into labor. Chuck rushed her to the hospital, but a mistake during the birth got the umbilical cord wrapped around the baby's neck, choking him as he was being born. It was a tragic mistake.

Chuck and Jackie cried once again at the loss of another child.

Chuck was offered the chance to go back out to Nevada the following year. He jumped at the chance because he was anxious to do something other than mechanical drawings. However, this time the government wasn't allowing families to come out with the volunteers. Chuck and Jackie agreed that Chuck should go, if for nothing more than to get away from a job that he didn't really enjoy for a few months.

Rather than driving west, Chuck was able to take a charter flight from Knoxville.

He participated in Operation Hardtack II that summer. It was notable because there were thirty-seven detonations in just six weeks. Most of these were detonations with a much smaller yield than those of 1957. Two of the detonations actually had no radioactive release detected. The total yield of all the Hardtack II detonations was 45.8 kt as compared to the 74 kt detonation of the Hood Test in 1957. The lower-yield detonations reflected a growing concern over nuclear fallout.

Regardless, Chuck made sure to have his radiation badge checked regularly whenever he participated in a detonation.

Chuck had had enough of big bombs detonating and exposing him to radiation. He didn't want to continue to push his luck that he wouldn't get sick or worse from the exposure. When the opportunity came up to return to Nevada in 1959, he passed on it.

1959-1974
A FAKE WAR

Jackie gave birth to their second child Robert Caldwell in 1958 as Chuck looked for ways to take care of his growing family.

He continued to make his clay miniatures, but they were hard to sell because of the clay's softness. No one wanted a figurine that might sweat or sag if the room where it was displayed got too hot or bend in an odd shape if hit wrong.

Two years later, in 1960, Jackie and Chuck welcomed Shonna into the world and then John in 1965. Their children now had an age span of eleven years between them. Forty-three-year-old Jackie was having to change diapers even as she readied David for junior high.

Chuck added the basement to their South Tampa Lane home after Shonna's birth to have two more bedrooms for the children. The basement also provided them with a fallout shelter in case of an atomic bomb attack. In Oak Ridge in the 1960s, it was considered unusual if you didn't have a fallout shelter. The birthplace of the atomic bomb was well aware of the dangers of radioactive fallout.

The younger children started to grow old enough to attend, Elm Grove School, the elementary school was just a short walk through the trees behind the Caldwell house.

The 1960s was an interesting time to grow up in Oak Ridge. The city had incorporated in 1959 and was now an open community. Locally, it was a safe community, despite the fears that old-time residents had had about opening the gates. Nationally, though, people were worried about the Cold War becoming a very hot war.

David Caldwell remembers the old guard houses that still

stood even when he attended junior high school. Although the city of Oak Ridge was open to the public, there were still plenty of areas where the old fencing still stood, a reminder of Oak Ridge's top-secret days.

"I remember a warning horn that would sound off if there was some sort of accident at one of the labs," David said. "It had a sound like no other horn. When I heard it, it was no great panic, though. I guess if it had anything to do with radiation, it would have been well-deserved panic, but for us, it was just another day."

Where most places in the country, and even the world, feared what atomic energy could do, for Oak Ridgers it was no big deal.

The X-10 Graphite Reactor at the Oak Ridge National Laboratory had changed the world by creating plutonium-240, which was used in the atomic bomb. It was shut down in 1963. By 1966, it had been designated a National Historic Landmark by the U.S. Department of the Interior. Then in 1968 it was finally opened for the public to tour.

David remembers walking across a catwalk through a shutdown reactor. He could look down and see where the cooling water and radioactive rods would usually be. In the laboratories, you could put your hands in gloves that reached into a sealed room and manipulate the apparatus enclosed in the room. He had no fear of exposure to any residual radiation. It wasn't something that Oak Ridgers worried too much about.

While Oak Ridge was an incorporated city and the land privately owned, much of the land surrounding the city limits was still government owned. This meant that drivers weren't allowed to leave the main roads to explore the areas that had been reclaimed by nature. Kids will be kids, though. Teenagers would wander through the woods, sometimes stumbling across a fire hydrant amidst a grove of trees or rotted wood that seemed too straight in the way it was laid out to be natural.

"I remember biking back there at night," David said. "If you sit and let your eyes adjust, you could see a dull glow. We always thought that it was radioactive waste, but it turns out that it was just foxfire."

When the Caldwells had first moved to Oak Ridge, they had joined the Oak Ridge Presbyterian Church, one of two Presbyterian churches in town. However, Chuck became disenchanted with it because the church had members going to the homes of other members to explain why they needed to give money for the different programs at the church.

"I thought this isn't Christian," Chuck said.

So the Caldwells started attending the Covenant Presbyterian Church. The church had a smaller membership, but the Caldwells felt more at home there. Chuck also became very active, helping out where he could. One Christmas, he built a stable out of railroad ties so that a Nativity scene could be placed in it. Another time, he used a bulldozer to level out the top of a hill so that a baseball diamond could be built. He also organized three different women's basketball teams for the church although he didn't know anything about basketball.

South Tampa Lane where the Caldwells lived was a cul-de-sac and one of the few level streets in the neighborhood. On a warm night, you could look out and see fifteen to twenty neighborhood kids playing the street and yards.

"Anywhere there were three trees together, someone had built a tree house," Chuck said.

Jackie always made sure that her children had a tasty breakfast in the morning. When not caring for her four children, she always seemed to be sewing, knitting or reading her Bible.

David got his first paper route when he was twelve years old and was just as diligent as his father had been about making sure that the papers were delivered. He had more hills to bike up and down than his father had had with his paper routes. The weather was just as cold as Ohio in the winter, but David had a guardian angel to keep him from getting too cold.

"East Tennessee can get pretty cold in the winter," David said. "Sometimes it got so cold that Mom would start the car and take me to get the papers and drive me around to deliver them."

The Caldwells always seemed to have a pet or two around, usually a dog, but sometimes a dog and a cat. David once adopted a three-legged dog and the Caldwells kept him.

Another time, the family had an orange tabby that lived under the porch. She was pregnant and disappeared for a few days and David started to worry. Jackie told him that the cat had probably just gone off to have its kittens.

Three days later, his mother called David onto the porch and pointed out the orange tabby to him. She was carrying one of her kittens from the hedge to her usual place under the porch. Behind her, walked the Caldwell's dog at the time, a lab mix who was carrying another one of the kittens. The dog and cat made three trips back and forth to move all of the kittens.

Major Charles W. Caldwell of the First Tennessee Volunteer Infantry. Courtesy of Chuck Caldwell.

Chuck turned to his love of history and his art to help fight the tedium of his job making technical drawings. He organized a local Civil War roundtable, a group that met to talk about Civil War topics and listen to speakers make presentations on the war.

He also thought that members of the roundtable and other re-enactors in the area should get together and form their own company that could participate in the centennial re-enactment events that were quickly approaching.

"I missed the Battle of Bull Run, but I traveled to Shiloh in April of 1962 to be there on the battlefield for that," Chuck said.

While there, he got the idea to form a re-enacting unit that would represent East Tennesseans who had served in the war. He put together a meeting of all of the re-enactors in the Oak Ridge region and they sat down to talk about forming a re-enacting unit.

The first thing that they had to sort out was whether they would represent the Union or Confederacy. Although Tennessee had been a Confederate State, around 31,000 East Tennesseans had fought in the Union Army. The group decided to be a Confederate unit.

The next question the group considered was whether they would be part of the Western or Eastern Confederate Army. In the western army, they would be fighting under General Braxton Bragg. Also, there were only three Confederate Army units in the Eastern Army.

The group decided they wanted to fight under General Robert E. Lee in the Eastern Army. Then they had to choose whether they would represent the First Regiment, Seventh Regiment or Fifteenth Regiment.

The group voted to be the First Tennessee Infantry because the company had the nickname Mountain Boys, which seemed to fit Chuck's group well. The company organized in Winchester, Tennessee, in April 1861 under the command of Colonel Peter Turney. It included men from Grundy, Coffee, Franklin, Bedford, Moore, and Lincoln counties. The company fought with the Army of Northern Virginia from Seven Pines to Cold Harbor. At the Battle of Gettysburg, the company had had more than sixty percent casualties.

Chuck was pleased with the group's final choice because he felt he had a special connection with the unit, although he didn't realize just how special. One of his prized possessions was a battered foot locker that he had purchased from an antique shop in New Market, Virginia. It had once been owned by Colonel Turney.

Chuck and his group started to compile a roster of the names of the men who had fought with the First Regiment and Chuck was surprised.

"There were two Caldwells in C Company," Chuck said. "One was my great-grandfather Isaac Caldwell and the other was his brother, Andrew Jackson Caldwell. What are the odds that we would pick out, arbitrarily, the company that my great-grandfather had fought in?"

Chuck had known that his great-grandfather had been a Confederate soldier, but he hadn't realized that he had fought for the First Tennessee Volunteers until he had received the roster.

Isaac Caldwell had lived in Washington County and was described as being five feet nine inches tall with a dark complexion, black hair, and blue eyes.

Now Chuck's time as a re-enactor took on an even greater significance for him. He was doing more than just re-enacting history, he felt that he was building a connection with a great-grandfather whom he had never known.

One newspaper described Chuck re-enacting with the First Tennessee Infantry, saying, "Between two hills separating a fringe of giant oak trees from a field of rolling grass, a group of grey-clad soldiers burst into sight of a column of Yankee regulars. Leading the charge was a black-bearded Confederate major whose piercing rebel yell [heard] over the din of artillery and rifle fire."

"Smoke from hidden cannon made the men in grey seem like ghosts as they darted from tree to tree and rock to rock. Seemingly everywhere, the rebel major directed the attack with deliberate precision. Almost inevitably, the Blue ranks wavered—then broke before the whooping rebel troops. The major paused to speak to a wounded companion still proudly bearing a battle flag inscribed '1st Tennessee Volunteer Infantry Regiment.'"

The country began marking the anniversary of the Civil War in 1961. Unlike the last big anniversaries in the 1930s, no Civil War veterans were alive to be honored. The last one had died in 1956. The torch had been passed. Reunions were gone and had been replaced by re-enactors like Chuck.

He came to Gettysburg for the centennial events in 1963. It was also a battle where his great-grandfather had fought and been captured, which made it even more significant for Chuck. The group drove most of the way along U.S. Route 11, camping in state parks at nights. With thirty men, spending all their time together, tempers flared occasionally. One lieutenant consistently wanted to do his own thing rather than work with the group. The other men in the unit had enough at one point and busted the lieutenant back to private. He got mad and went home. Another re-enactor cut his foot so badly at one of the camps on the way to Gettysburg that he also had to return home.

The group eventually made it to Gettysburg. It was Chuck's first time back to the battlefield since 1938. Much had changed, but it was still full of history. He and David and about thirty other re-enactors from Tennessee had invaded north to once again fight the Yankees.

"I was proud to be there, but I felt there was something missing without the actual veterans there," Chuck said.

They camped near Seminary Ridge and ate and showered in the National Guard armory, a two-story art-deco style brick building constructed in 1938 by the Works Projects Administration. It had served for a short time as a prisoner-of-war camp for German prisoners during World War II.

David wasn't an official re-enactor, but he did enjoy spending the time with his father and learning the maneuvers. He and Chuck also spent many hours before the re-enactment making black-powder charges in the basement of their Oak Ridge home.

For their uniforms, Chuck's company had ordered cadet uniforms from West Point Military Academy and had replaced the buttons with ones from the Tennessee Highway Patrol, which had the state seal on them. Such uniforms wouldn't pass muster with modern re-enactors, but they were economical and served just fine for the centennial anniversary.

"We tried to be as salty looking as we could," Chuck said. "Uniforms now are exquisite. You could almost put them into a museum."

Chuck was one of 1,500 re-enactors who participated in a parade on July 2, which was reported as the largest parade crowd in twenty-five years. An estimated 35,000 to 50,000 people lined the parade route. It took nearly two hours to pass a given point. The participants marched east on West High Street to Baltimore Street, then north through the center of town and out Old Harrisburg Road. Air force jets flew overhead to accompany them.

The parade also included more than 5,000 members of the Pennsylvania National Guard and units of the Air Force, Navy, Coast Guard and Civilian Air Patrol. At the head of the parade, four Pennsylvania State Policemen rode on motorcycles and six state policemen rode on horseback accompanying a re-enactor playing President Abraham Lincoln.

"The Confederate troops provided excitement along the route of the parade by firing a cannon and by one unit firing volleys much as must have occurred a century ago when the Confederates swarmed into Gettysburg on July 1 to push out the Union troops holding the town that afternoon," the *Gettysburg Times* reported.

As the group walked around the circle in the center of town, Chuck heard someone in the crowd say, "What is that bedraggled outfit?"

Now Chuck knew their uniforms weren't perfect, but he believed that they were passable. Unlike modern re-enactors who strive to be historically accurate in their uniforms and equipment, re-enactors in the 1960s essentially just wanted to look the part. Few people would be able to spot the difference between brass buttons and plastic ones.

Before Chuck could reply to the heckler, someone behind him yelled out, "They're the First Tennessee Infantry, by God!"

Roughly the same amount of people came out to see the re-enactment of Pickett's Charge on July 3 as had come out for the parade. That was where Chuck had the most fun during his visit to Gettysburg. It thrilled him and left him feeling like he was actually part of the battle. However, no shots were fired on the field and there was no staged combat. "The cheering Confederate Grays came to a statuesque halt 50 feet from the stone wall and held their battle poses for the benefit of photographers on the sidelines and in their own ranks," the *Gettysburg Times* reported.

The entire scene from start to finish took only twenty minutes. When it ended, officers of the Union and Confederacy shook hands, and then raised the American flag on a flagpole at the Angle while the band played "The Star Spangled Banner."

While the First Tennessee had been chided for being bedraggled, at least they weren't wearing sunglasses like some of the Union soldiers were during the re-enactment.

Jackie and the younger children didn't share Chuck's enthusiasm for the Civil War, although they did attend the 100th anniversary of the Battle of Gettysburg with Chuck.

Years later, on another trip to Gettysburg, Chuck drove around explaining who the people who were portrayed by the different statues were, including John Burns, the sixty-nine-year-old civilian and veteran of the War of 1812, who took up arms to fight during the Battle of Gettysburg. When they came upon the Burns statue a second time, Chuck said, "Okay, Honey, who is this?"

Jackie shrugged and said, "Johnny Appleseed?"

Jackie had attended some of Chuck's early re-enacting events with him, but he thinks it was an event in Kentucky that turned her off re-enacting for good. Although families had been invited to attend with their husbands, the bathroom facilities consisted of a trench dug in the ground that had to be used by males and females alike.

Once, right before a family trip to a re-enactment, young John fell out of a tree and broke his arm. Of course, no one realized it until the next day when his fingers started going numb. Jackie quickly volunteered to stay home with her youngest child while Chuck and the others went to the re-enactment.

Jackie was more interested in Bible reading. Rather than attending re-enacting events, she liked to travel to Bible conferences in North Carolina and Georgia and listen to the speakers. Chuck enjoyed going with her to these events, but he still would have preferred re-enacting history.

Chuck had been a part of so much of the modern era, and yet, it was the past he longed for. At Gettysburg, he would be able to be a part of the battle in a way that he hadn't been able to do in 1938.

Chuck's unit participated in re-enactments throughout the centennial remembrances. In April 1965, they even marched the 110-mile route of Heth's Division from Petersburg, Virginia, to Appomattox Court House where Confederate General Robert E. Lee surrendered to Ulysses S. Grant.

Chuck's reputation as an artist outside of the Museum of Atomic Energy was growing. He competed in local shows and continued making his small miniatures from clay. He was one of two dozen artisans who formed the Foothills Craft Guild in 1967.

One day in November of 1966, Jackie brought him a block of something that looked similar to clay, but it was called Sculpey, a polymer clay originally developed to stop leaks from broken pipes. It didn't stop the leaks, but the inventor's wife was a sculptor and realized the polymer clay's artistic value.

"I was with Mary in Oak Ridge and we were looking at creative craft books and one of them said that with this type of clay, you could bake it and it would be permanent," Jackie told him.

Chuck was certainly interested. One problem with clay was that when it was in a warm area, it tended to sweat. He used to do All-American football players every year, but he couldn't display them for long because the oils would begin coming out of the clay and beading on the miniatures. The other problem was that clay didn't harden permanently, which meant that anything he created could easily be damaged if it was held too hard or accidentally hit something. A Sculpey figurine that had been baked could be dropped on the floor and not break or even chip.

Using Sculpey, Chuck began to create his miniature figures and bake them at 300 degrees for thirty minutes once he was satisfied with the way they looked. Then he would paint them and not have to worry about them being damaged.

"The first month I must have made 100 figures," Chuck said. "I just went crazy. I couldn't put it down."

Chuck begins each of his figures with research. One of his trademarks is the authenticity of the uniforms and equipment that his figures wear, whether it's a military uniform or an athletic team uniform, so he makes sure to find the needed sources to get things right.

He forms each figure's legs out of Sculpey first, and he leaves a wire hoop sticking out of the top. Then he connects the torso to the legs with the wire loop. Once the miniature is baked hard, he does a final inspection and shaves any areas that need final shaping. The final product is generally at a scale of six feet equals five inches.

Chuck in his Oak Ridge workshop with some of his figures in 1970. Courtesy of Chuck Caldwell.

The first figure that Chuck made from Sculpey was of a star Oak Ridge High School football player. He numbered this figure "#1". It became the first of more than 15,000 numbered miniatures.

"As a supreme test Chuck gave the first figurine to his children to play with. In his own words they (His children) 'Can dismantle a bowling ball.' The figurine survived," Fred Stewart wrote in *The Oak Ridger*.

In 1968, Chuck resigned from the Oak Ridge National Laboratory on July 4. The nation's Independence Day had become his Independence Day. By this time, his job title was health physics surveyor and he was required to test rooms contaminated by radiation. He felt like he was becoming a guinea pig.

Chuck had had enough of being exposed to radiation and doing drawings in which he had little interest. His desire had always been to be a full-time artist and Sculpey gave him a way to do that. He could create figures that were actually durable enough to sell.

"I wanted to see how much interest there was in my work," Chuck said.

Jackie was supportive of his decision even though her husband was giving up a solid job with good benefits. "His talent is a gift of God. He was born with it. He should share it with everybody. I'm glad he quit his salaried job. The family is with him," she said.

The following month, the Caldwells loaded up their Ford station wagon with camping gear, clothes, and snacks for the four kids. Some nights they planned on camping to enjoy a nice park and save money. Other nights they would spend in a hotel in order to get a good night's sleep on a bed.

As they set off on their vacation/job hunt, one of the first places they stopped was the Museum Division of the National Park Service in Washington, D.C. With Chuck now working for himself, he needed to line up clients wherever they presented themselves. He showed the National Park Service personnel samples of his work.

The staff was nice and impressed with his miniatures. Chuck was told to go home and fill out his civil service papers and he would be hired. He was surprised at how easy it had been for him to get another job.

Chuck wasn't looking for a full-time job, though. He wanted commissioned work.

He told them that he would have to think about it and he would get back to them. The job offer had caught Chuck off guard. He had just started out on his own and wanted to see what he could go, but steady work with the government would allow him to take care of his family.

As the Caldwells left the National Park Service, Chuck stopped next to a policeman and asked for the quickest way to get out of Washington D.C. and get on the highway headed north. The directions took the Caldwells through downtown Washington.

This was in mid-July 1968. The city was still reeling from six days of rioting following the assassination of Martin Luther King, Jr. on April 4. That had been the straw that broke the camel's back for many African Americans around the country.

As word of King's death had spread, crowds had begun to gather at Fourteenth and U streets in the heart of the African American community in Washington. The peaceful crowd had grown and had soon turned into a mob that had started breaking windows followed by looting.

Washington wasn't the only city that saw rioting following King's death, but it was the nation's capital so it attracted a lot of attention on the national news.

Other incidents had followed during the next few days. Police and firefighters had been attacked as they had tried to respond to calls for help. With the Washington D.C. police vastly outnumbered by the rioters, President Lyndon Johnson had called out 13,600 military troops. Marines had stood behind mounted machine guns on the Capitol steps while the U.S. Army Third Infantry had guarded the White House. Washington had appeared to be a city under siege.

"I had heard about the rioting on TV and the destruction

that occurred, but I hadn't expected to see all of the blackened buildings and wrecked cars," Chuck said. "Nobody was on the street."

By the time the rioting had ended twelve people had been killed, 1,097 injured, and 1,199 buildings had either been damaged or destroyed. The estimated property loss was $25 million (more than $170 million in 2015 dollars). Even for the businesses left untouched by the rioting, if they relied on tourist dollars, they also suffered. The loss to the tourist trade in April and May was estimated to be $40 million (nearly $273 million in 2015 dollars).

Chuck hurried through the city as fast as he could. He doubted that his Tennessee license plates would have been appreciated since King had been killed in Memphis, Tennessee.

The next stop on their trip was in Gettysburg. He stopped at a museum on Baltimore Street and carried his figures in to show the manager. The man purchased every one of the figures and told Chuck that he needed to see LeRoy E. Smith, who owned the Gettysburg Hotel, the Gettysburg Battlefield Tours, Jennie Wade House, Hall of Presidents, and several other businesses in town. He also published the *Civil War Times*, a magazine that he had started in 1963. Chuck also got a job to make figures of all of the U.S. Presidents for the Hall of Presidents.

"After that, I got real cocky," Chuck said. "I told myself this is so easy."

A stop in New York City yielded more orders and contacts. The art director at *Time* and *Life* Magazines borrowed five of his figures and put them on display at the Natural History Museum in New York City.

The Caldwells continued their journey north until they reached Cooperstown, New York, home of the Baseball Hall of Fame.

In Cooperstown, Chuck visited the Woods Baseball Store.

The owner bought up a lot of Chuck's baseball figures and told him to talk to Louis Busch Hager, a theatrical producer and member of the Anheuser Busch family. He was also the American Woodland Museum, which had opened it 1962. It was located on the Busch estate and featured exhibits on the nature and history of the area. Hager also happened to be the nephew of the man who owned the St. Louis Cardinals.

Chuck found Hager at his museum and showed him his baseball figures.

"Can you get me 100 figures by the World Series?" Hager asked him.

Now this was in late August 1968 and the series was due to be played in October. That gave Chuck less than two months to complete all of the figures. He thought that he could do it.

Then Hager threw Chuck a curve ball. He wanted all of the figures to be members of the St. Louis Cardinals. He didn't just want a couple figures of each player. He wanted five or ten of specific players, such as Stan Musial, Lou Brock, Orlando Cepeda, Mike Shannon, and Curt Flood. Hager wanted twenty figures each of pitcher Bob Gibson and catcher Tim McCarver. Finally, all of the figures had to be different.

Gibson had been the MVP of the 1967 World Series helping the Cardinals win three of their four games. He was still on fire in 1968. In fact, the Cardinals were still on fire. The team was far ahead in first place. The team had won the 1967 World Series against the Boston Red Sox in seven games. Everyone figured that they were a shoe in to win the 1968 World Series.

"Since they wanted the figures to all be different so one he might have a leg raised, another he might have his hat off, another had him in an away jersey," Chuck said.

He managed to make all of the figures in time, and as a bonus for his good work, Hager gave him two tickets to the World Series.

Unfortunately, the Cardinals lost the series against the Detroit Tigers in seven games. Gibson went 2-1 in the series. He had had an outstanding season going 22-9 with an ERA of 1.12. He also had 268 strikeouts, thirteen shutouts, and fifteen consecutive wins.

Chuck still came out the winner because Hager and Jack Willett decided to stage a one-day art show in New York City in January 1969 featuring Chuck's miniatures. The plan was that if all of the figures sold, Chuck would earn $13,000 (roughly $84,000 today).

In all of the excitement of making the baseball figures and going to the World Series, Chuck totally forgot about working for the National Park Service. While the trip had left the Caldwells with only $100 in the bank, it brought an immediate return of $500 in cash and lots of orders including the $1,000 commission for the Cardinals figures. The total value would allow him to at least match his annual income from the Oak Ridge National Laboratory.

Some of the individual orders that he spent time working on included a gun collector who wanted Chuck to make a figure holding each of the guns in his collection and dressed in an outfit to match the time period of the weapon, a woman who wanted a figure of her brother-in-law in his football uniform for William Jewell College in Missouri, and a figure of the president of Reichhold Chemical Company in New York.

One of Chuck's biggest disappointments during this time was a commission that didn't come to be, at least by him. He was commissioned to create a monument that would represent the State of Tennessee and the Civil War soldiers who fought at Gettysburg. He submitted the design, cost estimates, and all of the other paperwork that the group in charge of the monument wanted.

"They liked the design, but decided the monument should be done by a 'well-known' sculptor," Chuck said in an interview.

Because of such delays and indecision, there was no Tennessee monument at Gettysburg until 1982. The monument is a sixteen-foot-long polished stone rectangle with three stone stars atop it. It is engraved with information about the Tennesseans in the battles and a simple drawing of three soldiers.

Chuck continued his work for his various clients and developed some good relationships with them. He did a replica of the old Sportsman Park in St. Louis that contained 25,000 miniature people in the stands. These weren't his full-size miniatures, but tiny people less than an inch high, yet fully formed, just not as detailed. He did similar commissioned work for the New York Jets and Cleveland Browns.

When the Oak Ridge National Laboratory wanted a medallion for its Atomic Pioneer Award, it commissioned Chuck. Three medallions were made from gold at the Y-12 plant.

"It was the first medal of its kind and the only presentation of the award was made Feb. 27, 1970, at the White House by the President to James B. Conant, General Leslie Groves and Vannevar Bush, pioneers in the atomic field," according to *The Oak Ridger*.

Conant received the award for his work on the National Defense Research Committee. Groves had been in charge of Oak Ridge during its top secret years during the war. Bush had headed the Office of Scientific Research and Development in World War II.

By 1971, Chuck had served in two wars, survived large doses of radiation from multiple nuclear explosions, and lost two children. He had certainly prayed during those times, asking God to keep him alive through his trials. Yet, in all that time, while God did protect him, he never saw fit to actually speak to Chuck.

That was until May 3, 1971.

He and Jackie both smoked and had been trying to stop for a couple years. Both of them had been smoking for decades. It had been no big deal growing up. Of course, the warnings about the dangers of smoking started appearing in the 1960s, not that they needed someone to tell Chuck and Jackie, they could feel it in their bodies as they struggled for breath after minor exertions. They could see the yellowing of their light-colored clothing. Besides, Chuck had survived creosote and radiation, what was a little nicotine?

On a 1948 trip to New Orleans to watch Alabama play Texas, they had decided to quit smoking. It was a difficult trip as they had struggled hour by hour not to smoke even as the Crimson Tide had lost the game 27-7.

Their resolve didn't last and soon they were smoking again before they got back home to Oak Ridge. Eventually, Jackie was able to quit before Christmas 1970, but Chuck still craved his cigarettes.

Then on May 3, 1971, he was walking across his yard to his house. Halfway across, Chuck heard two words as clear as a bell. "Don't smoke." Chuck stopped walking and looked around. He was alone, but he had heard someone say those words. He waited for more, but he heard nothing else.

"I have never had an experience like that before or since," Chuck said. "God singled me out to tell me something. If God or the Son of God tells you don't smoke, man, you don't disobey that."

Chuck quit smoking and drinking from that time forward and his resolve has never wavered no matter how stressful life has gotten.

LeRoy Smith invited Chuck to come up to Gettysburg and open up a studio in 1972. The idea appealed to Chuck and he came up for the summer to try it out and see how many figures he could sell.

When Chuck arrived in Gettysburg, LeRoy took him out to a building on Baltimore Street where LeRoy's son in law had a shop where he baked cookies that he sold to the tourists. LeRoy told him that he could have the whole basement of the shop to use as a studio.

The problem was that Hurricane Agnes had blown through earlier in the year, bringing flooding and worse all along the East Coast and even inland areas such as Gettysburg. Although the standing water in the basement was gone, it was still a long way from being dry.

"When I stepped on the stone squares that made up the floor, water seeped up between the cracks," Chuck said.

Chuck said that he couldn't work there and LeRoy agreed so he offered Chuck a room above the store. It had a toilet, a sink, and a small stove for heating up food. Chuck could make his figures and live in the room rent free. The only condition was that he had to guard the downstairs at night.

Living conditions were a little rough, but Chuck did well that year. He also got to live at the site of his favorite Civil War battle for months.

Chuck and Jackie's oldest son, David, had graduated high school in 1970 and was working in a grocery store as an assistant manager. He was in line to be the next store manager, but the owner of the small chain of stores was "mercurial" and David began to wonder if he would get the position and if he even wanted it.

The Vietnam War was still going on. So far, David hadn't been drafted and he knew that could change at any time. He decided he wanted to join the Marine Corps like his father had so he visited the enlistment office in September of 1972 and signed up and took the physical.

When he came home, he told his parents he had just taken a physical.

"Your physical for what?" Chuck asked him.

"The Marines," David replied.

Chuck was shocked. His son had never shown interest in joining the military. David didn't know what he had signed up for.

"I thought to myself, 'They're going to kill this kid,'" Chuck said. However, he didn't tell David that. Instead, he said, "My advice is to keep your mouth shut and do what they say, when they say it."

So David shipped off to Parris Island just as his father had thirty-one years earlier. He dutifully wrote to his parents every week as they wondered whether he would be sent to Vietnam.

It was a rough time for David, especially since his drill instructor made it that way. It began with his arrival on Parris Island. A bulldog of a man stepped onto the Greyhound bus. It was late at night and all of the recruits on the bus were tired and some were hungover.

The Marine sergeant said in an even, calm voice, "Gentlemen, I'd like to welcome you to Parris Island. This will be your home for the next thirteen weeks. Now when I give the word, I want you to go out and stand on those footprints."

The footprints are painted yellow on the cement in front of the receiving building. They are spaced so that once the recruits are standing on them, they will be standing four abreast. They will also be standing with their feet in the correct position to be at attention. The footprints have been a Parris Island tradition since the 1960s.

Suddenly, the sergeant's calm demeanor changed and he screamed, "Move!"

"People were going out the windows to get away from him," David said.

During training, David saw recruits hit and kicked for minor infractions. David answered a question wrong in his senior rifle class and the drill instructor smacked him on the head with the butt of the rifle.

"If he came through the door right now, I'd be looking for

something to whack him over the head with because of the way he treated us," David said.

When he graduated boot camp, his platoon was the first platoon in years that hadn't been sent to Vietnam as replacement troops. Had David graduated a week earlier, it would have been a different story.

David was sent to the Second Medical Battalion. It was an unusual mix of sailors and Marines. Since the Marines were in the Department of the Navy, Navy medical personnel provided the care for the Marines. His battalion had a Navy commanding officer, a naval executive officer, two companies of naval personnel, and two companies of Marines. David decided that he liked medical work so much that he got an interservice transfer to the become part of the Navy Medical Corps.

The next year, David was on leave from the Marine Corps and he drove his father up to Gettysburg in the spring to set up his shop.

Well, LeRoy Smith was going through a bad divorce. He had turned over the ownership of the Old Gettysburg Village to Seamus Garry and Garry had rented out the place where Chuck had stayed the prior year.

Seamus offered him a small space in a building that looked like a five-sided outhouse next to a man who was making Minié balls. It was an open area that offered Chuck no place where he could display his miniatures for sale.

Chuck turned to David and said, "Let's go home."

They got back in the car and David drove them back to Tennessee, and Chuck didn't return to Gettysburg for eight years.

His life had other highways that he needed to travel first.

1974-2016
LOTS OF CLAY SOLDIERS

Bob Cowan made Chuck an offer he couldn't refuse. Bob was one of Chuck's best customers. He would call Chuck from his gallery in Texas and place regular orders for Chuck's miniature figures.

Then one day he called Chuck and asked him to come to Texas to do a one-man show at the gallery. Chuck drove down to Dallas to prepare his figures for display and sale and it turned into a successful show.

"Would you consider moving to Dallas and working with my shop?" Bob asked him at the conclusion of the show.

Chuck went back to Oak Ridge and talked it over with Jackie. Since Chuck was on his own, nothing was holding the Caldwells to Oak Ridge so in 1974, the Caldwells packed up and moved to Lake Dallas, thirty-two miles northwest of Dallas.

While Chuck and Jackie adjusted to the move easily, Bobby, Shonna, and John didn't like it so much. Oak Ridge had been the only home they had known and they had to leave it and all their friends behind to move to Texas.

Chuck began producing his miniatures and selling them through Cowan's gallery called The Militaria.

Chuck also got a job creating circus performers and animals for the Howard Brothers Circus, a one-sixteenth life scale model of the Ringling Bros. and Barnum & Bailey Combined Shows, exact down to the smallest details. Although not a circus performer himself, Howard Tibbals had been a fan of the circus since his childhood. In 1956, he began building what would become his lifetime passion, a scale circus. Such an undertaking required help and Tibbals had seen Chuck's work while he was still at the University of Alabama and remembered him when he started to put together a miniature circus. Tibbals could build the miniature wagons and tents, but he needed Chuck to make the performers and animals for him.

Although it was first displayed in 1965, Tibbals had continued adding to it, which is why he asked for Chuck's help.

Chuck would drive to Florida and spend a couple months working on site. Jackie and the kids went with him.

Although Chuck liked Tibbals, his direct supervisor was a man who had a temper and was never happy. Tibbals was pleased with the work, though. The miniature circus was displayed as part of a museum exhibit in Washington, D.C., and it was part of the Knoxville World's Fair in 1982. Today, it is part of the John and Mabel Ringling Museum of Art in Florida.

Things were going well for Chuck until Cowan sold his shop in 1976. The new owners still sold miniature figures but they bought ones that were factory produced. Chuck suddenly found himself with no outlet to sell his figures.

He and Jackie looked around for work, but had no luck. They kept getting told that they were too qualified for the jobs they applied for, which frustrated Chuck. Too qualified should have meant that he was a great applicant for the position.

Then a company that created and manufactured school rings, team rings, and championship rings opened virtually across the street from the Caldwell's home in Lake Dallas. Chuck found out that the company needed a sculptor and he thought that it would be the perfect job for him.

"I brought in my samples, and they were very excited about it," Chuck said. "They were asking me questions about when I could start work."

Chuck was taken on a tour of the company and even shown where he would be working. The final stop was at the human resources office where he was asked to fill out some final paperwork. Chuck watched the young human resources director read down the information that Chuck had filled out. Suddenly, the man got a shocked look on his face.

Chuck had been watching the human resources director's progress down the page of information and the change in attitude came where Chuck had written down his date of birth in 1923.

"I'll never forget that expression," Chuck said. "I could almost see him backing off."

Then the man looked up and said, "We'll give you a call back."

And he never heard back from the company.

Jackie finally wound up with a job cleaning houses. She was certainly too qualified for that, but at least she had paying work. She was working for a lady who attended the same church as the Caldwells. Chuck never understood why the woman worked at all. Her husband was an inventor who had made a lot a money so they certainly didn't need the money that the woman was making.

Chuck continued working on his figures as he looked for new work.

"It was a miserable time," Chuck said. "I call them the dark years, never thought about quitting and going to day job."

When Chuck asked Jackie about her work once, she told him, "Why don't you come along? It's great fun."

He wasn't sure if she was being sarcastic or not, but he did go along to help her and the two of them had fun cleaning together.

When the woman Jackie was working for did finally decide to give up cleaning houses, she turned the business over Jackie. Chuck started going along with her to help her in her weekly cleaning of the half a dozen houses.

One of the places that Jackie cleaned was a bank. Together, Chuck and Jackie would have the place sparkling in fifteen to twenty minutes. They also cleaned the house of the Greenville

Superintendent of Schools. This house presented some problems for Chuck since the superintendent's wife wanted him to clean the outside of the kitchen windows.

"The only way to get to them was through a bunch of tall bushes," Chuck said. "It took me forever to get to them and I kept getting pricked."

Things began changing in 1975. The Franklin Mint contacted Chuck and asked him to do a series of twelve figures called "People of the Canada."

The Franklin Mint is a private mint that was founded in 1964 when it began striking legal tender coins for foreign countries. This soon spread to creating collectibles from die-cast models, games, and dolls. By the 1970s, the Franklin Mint's reputation for beautiful and sought after collectibles was already established.

Chuck's original miniatures for the "People of the Canada" series would be cast in pewter and sold as a collectible series limited to 2,800 sets. The best part was that Chuck would be paid $1,000 per figure. This job alone would pay him nearly sixty percent of the average family income in 1975.

He jumped at the chance. He flew to Philadelphia where he sculpted the figures.

This marked the beginning of the end for the "Dark Years."

Chuck soon got a job with the Greenville Natural History Museum creating prehistoric sea creatures in Lucite pools. He found the work interesting and he even learned a lot about prehistoric life.

The Franklin Mint called Chuck again in 1976 and asked him to do another series called "The Old West." This time, he was paid $2,000 per figure for a series of eight figures cast in bronze.

"I was so excited that I went into my backyard and began marking off where I wanted to put my pool because I had always wanted a pool," Chuck said.

Chuck never did get the pool, but he did take the job. He would fly to the Franklin Mint on Monday, work until Thursday night when he would fly home again so he could watch his son, Robert, play football on Friday night. After all, he was living in Texas where football was king and Chuck was a loyal subject.

With this assignment, Chuck and Jackie decided that they had made it through their hard times and Jackie quit cleaning houses for other people.

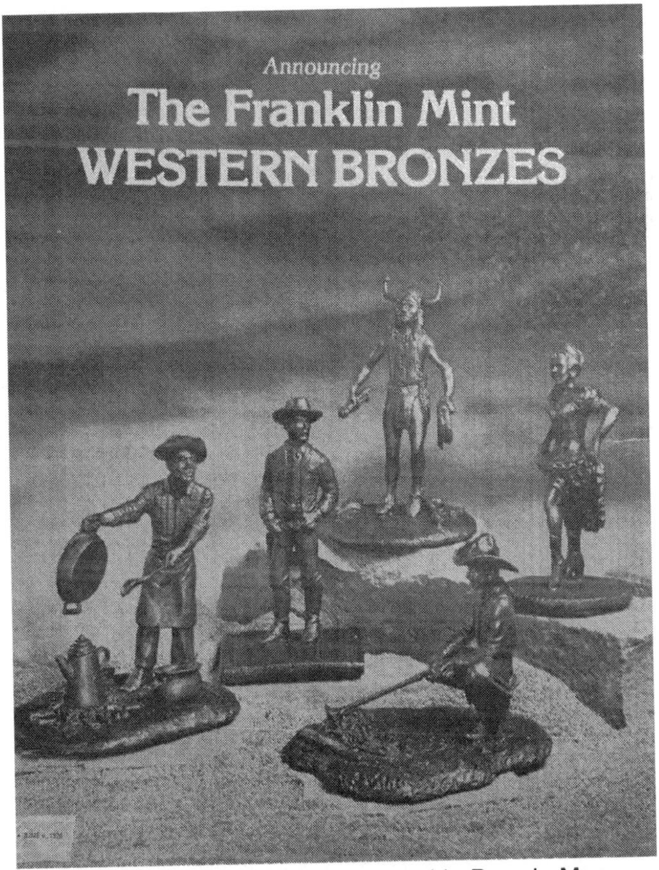

Part of a two-page ad that appeared in Parade Magazine for Chuck's second series with the Franklin Mint. Courtesy of Chuck Caldwell.

In 1981, Gettysburg pulled Chuck back once again when he had the chance to open his own studio near where he had worked in 1972. He traveled up to Gettysburg in April to open his studio in the Old Gettysburg Village shops at the beginning of the tourist season and stayed through October.

Like 1972, it was a successful venture and he decided to return the following year. This time Jackie came with him. She stayed with him for the summer and Chuck remained until he closed for the season in early October.

He had considered staying through the winter because he loved being in Gettysburg, but he missed Jackie and wanted to be with her. He would talk to himself on his morning walks debating the pros and cons.

"Eventually I decided I won either way and I went home," Chuck said.

After three successful years in Gettysburg, the Caldwells decided it was time to make a permanent move to Gettysburg. Nothing was anchoring them in Lake Dallas and Gettysburg had continued to attract Chuck time and again since he was fourteen years old.

The Caldwells rented an apartment on Baltimore Street that overlooked the courtyard Gettysburg Village Shops and put their house in Texas on the market. Chuck, Jackie, Shonna, and John moved to Gettysburg permanently. Chuck enjoyed the apartment because he could look down and see whether there were any tourists in the courtyard. If there weren't any, he could delay walking downstairs to open up his shop for the day.

Because he spent long days in his shop, Chuck would get his exercise in the mornings before he opened up. He would take a two-and-a-quarter-mile walk onto Culp's Hill where the Twenty-Ninth Ohio had fought, and then he would walk back and open the shop for the day.

Visitors would stop by to talk and watch Chuck work.

Many of them would leave behind a baseball cap which Chuck would hang from his ceiling crowded with dozens of hats.

He never did any advertising, but word of his creations spread and the shop became a regular stop for many annual visitors to Gettysburg. Chuck kept track of his customers' hometowns. He put up a large world map in the shop and would stick pins in the cities where his customers visited from. Eventually he had pins sticking in every state in the U.S. and fifteen different countries.

Chuck's shop in the Old Gettysburg Village. Courtesy of Chuck Caldwell.

After his divorce, Chuck's father had eventually remarried and found happiness again. When George Caldwell had retired, he had moved to Florida. He died in 1986 at the age of ninety-four. The rest of Chuck's family was still in good health and he got to see them at his father's funeral.

Although living in Gettysburg, a Civil War mecca, Chuck added WWII miniatures to the types of figures that he regularly sculpted. He had experienced a growing demand for them with the approach of the fiftieth anniversary of the World War II in the early 1990s. He set a goal for himself to do figures from every country that was involved in the war.

In 1992, he donned his Civil War uniform once again and joined hundreds of other re-enactors who served as extras in the movie *Gettysburg*. He spent eleven weeks filming scenes for the movie, although he says that he is not visible in any of the scenes of the final movie.

While shooting scenes out on Pumping Station Road, he was part of the Fifteenth Alabama as they were filmed charging time and again. Initially, the soldier actors used rubber bayonets, but the bayonets kept wobbling when the soldiers charged. It was decided that they would use real bayonets on the rifles during the charging scene.

Chuck played one of the casualties in the scene. As the company charged down the hill, he had to fall as if he had been shot. He managed his fall so that he landed near a sapling. The tree would block the soldiers coming behind him so that they wouldn't accidentally run over Chuck.

While Chuck was laying still and not moving, another extra dressed as a Union soldier approached his position at a run. The man tripped over a tree root and went sprawling right next to Chuck.

"Are you hurt?" Chuck whispered.

"No, but turn your head to the left," the other man whispered.

Chuck knew that he wasn't supposed to move, but it must have been important for him to have been asked to turn his head.

Chuck slowly turned his head in that direction and saw that the other man's bayonet had stuck in the ground right next to Chuck's head. Another inch and Chuck would have become a real casualty of the mock battle.

Near the end of the filming Jeff Daniels, who played Colonel Joshua Lawrence Chamberlain in the movie accidentally stepped on Chuck's ankle.

All in all, Chuck had a lot of fun filming the movie. Given the scope of the movie and the effects used, Chuck often felt like he was fighting the Civil War.

Many of the cast members also visited Caldwell's Originals while in Gettysburg.

"Tom Berenger bought a lot of figures and dioramas and other stuff and gave them as gifts to other members of the cast," Chuck said.

Gettysburg the movie was Chuck's last stint as a re-enactor. He had been re-enacting on and off since September 1962 and the centennial anniversary of the Battle of Antietam in Sharpsburg, Maryland.

Robert Caldwell became the third member of the family to join the military in 1990. He enlisted in the U. S. Navy at age thirty two. When the recruitment officer found out that Robert was a carpenter, he tried to get him to enlist in the Seabees.

The Seabees are the Navy's Construction Battalion. They build the bases, roads, and airstrips for the Navy, and Robert was a natural fit with them. The problem was that Robert would have to sign up for a seven-year enlistment. He wasn't sure that he wanted that so he opted for a regular enlistment of four years.

He was assigned to duty on the aircraft carrier, *U. S. S. Kitty Hawk* and went on to serve in Operation Desert Shield. Chuck and Jackie got a chance to visit him and tour the ship while it was in port.

Chuck's mother had remarried shortly after her divorce in 1951. Her second husband had been a family friend of the Caldwells who was a widower. By the 1990s, she was living in a nursing home in Port Charlotte, Florida. She died in 1999 at age ninety-six, leaving Chuck an orphan at the age of seventy-three.

Barbara had been widowed at the end of World War II. She

had remarried Bill Drake and had three children with him. She was a happy grandmother in the 1990s. However, after her mother died, it was discovered that she had breast cancer and she died only a few years after her mother.

In 2000, Chuck and Jackie bought a house in Gettysburg near where Chuck and David had camped for the Battle of Gettysburg centennial in 1963. It quickly filled up with mementos of Chuck and Jackie's lives. Pictures of family were hung on the walls. Chuck's miniatures were placed in display cases. Jackie's Bibles sat on the bookshelves.

They were happy together.

Then in 2007, Jackie said that she wasn't feeling well and asked to go to the hospital.

"She was someone who always took care of herself, so I knew if she felt she needed to go to the hospital, something was really wrong," Chuck said.

After three days of observation, the doctors told Chuck that his wife's blood pressure was very low and that her body wasn't circulating enough blood.

The doctors allowed her to return home since there was nothing they could do. Her heart was working as best it could, but it wasn't enough.

Jackie died of congestive heart failure a week later at home with her family.

Jackie and Chuck had been married for sixty-two years and raised four children together. Her death devastated Chuck, but he continued on with the help of family and friends.

He closed his studio in town on the day Jackie died. He decided that he wanted to enjoy the rest of his life. He didn't give up sculpting, though. He worked from home in semi-retirement.

Family members weren't the only people Chuck was losing. The Marines who had served with him during World War

II, the men from the Nevada Test Site, friends from Orrville and Oak Ridge, were aging and dying.

Chuck stopped going to his WWII Marine reunions in 2010 because there were so few veterans who could attend that it just didn't seem like a time for rejoicing with old friends.

Time was marching on.

2016
A FULL CIRCLE

Chuck Caldwell's aged, but still nimble, fingers rolled the Sculpey modeling clay around until the friction from the motion made it was soft and easy to manipulate. He formed it into an arm raised in a salute. Then he attached it to a body that he had already formed and mounted on a small wooden platform.

Next came the head and the face. He cut a piece from the Sculpey block and began rolling it around between his palms. The face is the most-difficult part of each figure. Get the feet too big or the arms too short and no one was likely to notice, but set the eyes to close together or use the wrong shade of paint for the hair color and people would be telling him about it for years.

It doesn't look right. It's not alive.

Shape it, bake it, and bring it to life like the story of the Gingerbread Boy. True it was only a story, but within the story, truth can be found. The heat of the kiln bakes the Sculpey to a hardness that would last.

At ninety-two years old, Chuck is still healthy and living on his own in Gettysburg. Creosote. Tobacco. War. Radiation. None of these things had killed him, but they had served as the heat in the kiln that was his life.

He still visits with friends and hosts holidays for his family, which has grown to include four grandchildren and two great-grandchildren.

His house is full of memories. When he finishes creating one of his clay soldiers, it might be sold to a collector or Chuck might simply place it on one of the shelves in his dining room. One wall of the dining room is covered with shelves. They hold hundreds of five-inch-tall soldiers, athletes, musicians, and odd characters.

Chuck's WWII seabag marked with all of the places that he visited in the Pacific during the war. It sits packed with all of his Marine clothing in his basement. From the author's collection.

Over the years, Chuck has created more than 15,000 custom, individual figures (and that is only counting the ones made from Sculpey). Only these few hundred still remain in his possession. Most of the models are long dead, but standing on the shelf in Chuck's house, they live in that moment of time in which he captured them.

When Chuck closes his eyes, they come alive for him. He can see General George Pickett leading his famous charge at Gettysburg, Glenn Miller conducting his orchestra on "Moonlight Serenade," or a young Joe Namath leading the Crimson Tide to its 1964 National Football Championship. He can remember their stories, too.

He even has figures of Jackie in her WAVES uniform and three of himself in various Marine uniforms.

"Those I'm taking to the grave with me," he said.

His basement workshop is filled with other mementos. Caps given to him by customers at his studio store hang from the ceiling joists. Weapons from his time as a Marine and a Civil War re-enactor are mounted on the wall besides maps and pictures. His old canvas seabag sits under a worktable, packed up of clothing and with all of the places Chuck had visited during WWII stenciled on the side. It's almost as if he is ready to answer the call to serve one more time.

Books on the shelves are marked up with corrections or simply underlined where a person Chuck knew is written about. Nearly all of those people are dead now.

Surprisingly, when Chuck attended his seventieth Orrville High School reunion in 2011, nine members of his seventy-six-student graduating class were in attendance. Every boy in his class went into the service and six of the girls had served as nurses, WAVES and WACS during the war. In the two years following the reunion, sadly, two of those graduates died.

The seventy-fifth anniversary of WWII begins in 2016. Of the more than sixteen million Americans who served in WWII, less than a million are still alive and even fewer still will be alive in 2020 when the WWII anniversary ends. During the anniversary years, though, those men and women who are still alive will be recognized at ceremonies and reunions similar to the seventy-fifth anniversary of the Battle of Gettysburg.

Chuck will probably attend some of them just as he has in the past. It's likely that he will meet many young men who were the same age that he was in 1938 when he met the Civil War veterans attending the seventy-fifth anniversary of the Battle of Gettysburg. Things have come full circle and he has fulfilled his youthful wish.

Chuck has become a part of history.

Charles "Chuck" Caldwell

To Ron
Thank You

CHUCK CALDWELL
MARINE

NOTES

The Last Reunion

3 *Waking in coop:* Charles Caldwell, interviews with the author, 2014-2016. Because of the number of interviews conducted with Chuck Caldwell between 2015 and 2016, they will be referred to as if they were a single interview.

4 *Drive to Gettysburg:* Charles Caldwell, interviews with the author.

4 *First paved highway*: "History," *Nebraska Lincoln Byway*, Nebraska Tourism Commission, *LincolnHighwayNebraskaByway.com http://lincolnhighwaynebraskabyway.com/history* (accessed August 26, 2015).

4 *Gettysburg facts:* "Ten Facts About Gettysburg, July 1-3, 1863," Civil War Trust, *http://www.civilwar.org/battlefields/gettysburg/assets/ten-facts-about/ten-facts-about-gettysburg.html* (accessed August 26, 2015).

5 *First visit to Gettysburg*: Charles Caldwell, interviews with the author.

5 *Pennsylvania Memorial*: *Fiftieth Anniversary of the Battle of Gettysburg, Report of the Pennsylvania Commission* (Harrisburg, PA: William Stanley Ray, State Printer, 1913), 24.

6 *"Mighty, mighty severe":* Charles Caldwell, interviews with the author.

6 *Laughing in the car*: Charles Caldwell, interviews with the author.

6 *Valley Forge*: Charles Caldwell, interviews with the author.

6 *Climbing the hill:* Charles Caldwell, interviews with the author.

7 *Isaac Caldwell*: Diana Loski, "A World War II Veteran Remembers," *The Gettysburg Experience*, July 2014, 25;

7 *Archer's Brigade fighting*: Tim Smith, "The First Day at Gettysburg: Then and Now," Civil War Trust, *http://www.civilwar.org/battlefields/gettysburg/gettysburg-2011/gettysburg-then-and-now.html* (accessed October 16, 2015).

7 *1930s veterans*: Unsigned article, "Camp Aftermath," The Frank N. Britchner Collection scrapbook is part of the Adams County (Pa.) Historical Society collection. It is part of a donation by a pharmacist who lived in Gettysburg at the time of the fiftieth reunion of the Battle of Gettysburg. The scrapbook is a collection of articles written during the 1913 and 1938 reunions. Many come from the *Baltimore American*, but many others have been clipped from the newspaper and so the origin is

uncertain.

8 *Veteran mementos*: Charles Caldwell, interviews with the author.

8 *Veteran correspondence*: Charles Caldwell, interviews with the author.

8 *Veterans arrive*: Unsigned article, "Plans Completed for Gettysburg's Big Celebration," *The* (Beaver County, PA) *Daily Times*, June 28, 1938, 1.

9 *Gettysburg appearance*: Annette Tucker, "The Gettysburg Reunion – 1938," unpublished manuscript at the Adams County Historical Society, 3; Unsigned article, "Flags, Bunting Brighten Town for Battle Fete," *The Gettysburg Times*, June 23, 1938, 1.

9 *Tim Murphy*: Unsigned article, "Flags, Bunting Brighten Town for Battle Fete," June 23, 1938.

9 *Sleeping in coop*: Charles Caldwell, interviews with the author.

12 *Planning starts*: Stan Coben, *Hands Across the Wall: The 50th and 75th Reunions of the Gettysburg Battle* (Charleston, WV: Pictorial Histories Publishing Co., 2011), 40-1.

12 *Leonard Shealer*: Jess Haines, "95-year-old remembers role in 75th, 1938 reunion," *The Gettysburg Times*, June 30, 2012, 1.

13 *Camp set up*: Unsigned article, "Many People Visit College During Celebration," *The Gettysburg College Bulletin*, October 1938, 2.

13 *Flag display*: Tucker, "The Gettysburg Reunion – 1938", 3.

13 *Tent set up*: Tucker, "The Gettysburg Reunion – 1938", 5-6.

13 *Thrill to see both armies together*: Charles Caldwell, interviews with the author.

14 *William W. Banks*: Unsigned article, "Veteran Asks Permission to Remain at Gettysburg Until 'Gabriel Shall Call Us'," Unknown publication, July 7, 1938. This newspaper clipping is part of the 75th anniversary folder in the vertical files of the Adams County Historical Society.

14 *Close to 100 years old*: Charles Caldwell, interviews with the author.

14 *John Stonesifer*: Abbey Zelko, "Gettysburg tourist recalls experience at 75th anniversary: Gettysburg 150," PennLive.com, *http://www.pennlive.com/midstate/index.ssf/2013/06/gettysburg_tourist_recalls_exp.html* (accessed January 7, 2015).

14 *Chuck meeting veterans*: Charles Caldwell, interviews with the author.

15 *"...bullet thudded into Smith's cheek"*: Unsigned article, "Veterans of North and South Recall Gettysburg," *The* (Circleville, Ohio) *Daily Herald*, June 30, 1938, 3.

15 *2,000 umbrellas*: Unsigned article, "Here and There With the Veterans," *The Gettysburg Compiler*, July 9, 1938, 4.

15 *Henry Rogers*: Unsigned article, "Here and There With the Veterans," *The Gettysburg Times*, July 1, 1938, 1.

16 *Reverend John M. Claypool*: Unsigned article, "Here and There With the Veterans," July 9, 1938.
16 *Chuck visiting the camps*: Charles Caldwell, interviews with the author.
16 *Shrapnel ruins Gillette's britches*: Unsigned article, "Here and There With the Veterans," July 1, 1938.
17 *O. Richard Gillette*: Unsigned article, "Blue and Gray Relive Battle In Memories," *Syracuse Herald*, June 30, 1938, 1.
17 *Drinking with Gillette:* Charles Caldwell, interviews with the author.
17 *Gillette newsreel interview*: John McDonough, "Remembering Last Reunion of Civil War Veterans," NPR, *http://www.npr.org/templates/story/story.php?storyId=106259780* (accessed August 27, 2015).
18 *Roosevelt arrives*: Coben, *Hands Across the Wall,* 44.
19 *Collapsing from heat exhaustion*: Unsigned article, "President Roosevelt Dedicates Eternal Light Memorial to Cause of Peace Before 200,000 as Climax to 75th Anniversary of Civil War Battle," *The Gettysburg Times*, July 4, 1938, 1.
19 *Roosevelt's address*: Unsigned article, "Text of President's Address at 'Peace Light' Dedication," *The Gettysburg Times*, July 4, 1938, p. 1.
20 *Unveiling the memorial:* Unsigned article, "President Roosevelt Dedicates Eternal Light Memorial to Cause of Peace Before 200,000 as Climax to 75th Anniversary of Civil War Battle," 1.

Orrville

21 *Learning to curse*: Charles Caldwell, interviews with the author.
22 *Penney Farms*: "Penney Farms, Florida," Penney Farms Government, *http://www.penneyfarmsfl.govoffice2.com* (accessed August 31, 2015); "James Cash Penney," Find a Grave, *http://www.findagrave.com/cgi-bin/fg.cgi?page=gr&GRid=803* (accessed October 23, 2015).
22 *Pew climber*: Charles Caldwell, interviews with the author.
23 *Drawing cars*: Charles Caldwell, interviews with the author.
24 *Clay for gifts*: Charles Caldwell, interviews with the author.
24 *School at Penney Farms*: Charles Caldwell, interviews with the author.
24 *First Presbyterian Church*: Ben Douglass, "History of Wayne County, Ohio, from the days of the Pioneers and First Settlers to the Present Time," Orrville.com, *http://www.orrville.com/DEPT/SSD/HISTORY1.HTM* (accessed August 31, 2015).
26 *Orrville home*: Charles Caldwell, interviews with the author.
26 *Orrville history*: "History of Orrville," Orrville.com, *http://www.orrville.com/HISTORY.HTM* (accessed August 31, 2015).

27 *Orrville businesses*: Bob Witmer, *Orrville, Ohio, Historical Walking Guide* (Orrville, OH: Orrville YMCA, 1989), 50.

27 *Orrville population*: "Orrville, Ohio," Wikipedia, *http://en.wikipedia.org/wiki/Orrville,_Ohio* (accessed August 31, 2015); "Penney Farms, Florida

27 *Schools*: Mollie B. Curie on behalf of the Orrville Historical Society, *Images of America: Orrville* (Charleston, SC: Arcadia Publishing, 2012), 89; "History of Orrville," Orrville.com.

28 *Playing on a pond*: Charles Caldwell, interviews with the author.

28 *Toy soldiers*: "A Brief History of Toy Soldiers," The Toy Soldier Company, *http://www.toysoldierco.com/resources/toysoldierhistory.htm* (accessed August 31, 2015); Witmer, *Orrville, Ohio, Historical Walking Guide,* 15.

28 *Orrville football*: Witmer, *Orrville, Ohio, Historical Walking Guide,* 17.

29 *Melvin Horst*: "Melvin Charles Horst," Charley Project, *http://www.charleyproject.org/cases/h/horst_melvin.html* (accessed August 31, 2015); Curie, *Images of America: Orrville*, 122; Witmer, *Orrville, Ohio, Historical Walking Guide,* 34.

31 *Grandfather marries aunt*: Charles Caldwell, interviews with the author.

31 *Baseball card collecting*: "1933 Goudey Baseball Cards," Cardboard-Connection.com, *http://www.cardboardconnection.com/1933-goudey-baseball-cards* (accessed August 31, 2015).

32 *Baseball cards stolen*: Charles Caldwell, interviews with the author.

32 *1933 World's Fair*: "Official Guide Book World's Fair 1934," Butkus.org, *http://www.butkus.org/information/worlds_fair_1934/worlds_fair_1934.htm,* (accessed August 31, 2015); Robert W. Rydell, "Century of Progress Exposition," Encyclopedia of Chicago History, *http://www.encyclopedia.chicagohistory.org/pages/225.html* (accessed August 31, 2015).

33 *Graf Zeppelin*: "Graf Zeppelin History," Airships.net, *http://www.airships.net/lz127-graf-zeppelin/history* (accessed August 31, 2015).

33 *U.S.S. Akron and U.S.S. Macon*: "U.S.S. Akron (ZRS-4) and U.S.S. Macon (ZRS-5)," Airships.net, *http://www.airships.net/us-navy-rigid-airships/uss-akron-macon* (accessed August 31, 2015).

34 *Akron airdock*: Akron-Summit County Public Library, Summit Memory; "A Nine Acre Nest For Dirigibles," *Popular Science Month-*

ly, September 1929, 20.

34 *Ten football games*: Charles Caldwell, interviews with the author.

35 *Its own weather:* "Goodyear Airdock," Akron, Ohio, Library, *sc.akronlibrary.org/files/2011/11/73002259.pdf* (accessed August 31, 2015); Charles Caldwell, interviews with the author.

35 *Akron and Macon accidents*: "U.S.S. Akron (ZRS-4) and U.S.S. Macon (ZRS-5)," Airships.net.

35 *Sky Ride:* "Sky Ride and Hall of Science," Printmag.com, *http://www.printmag.com/wp-content/uploads/COP-bklt-005.jpg (*accessed August 31, 2015); "Official Guide Book World's Fair 1934," Butkus.org, *http://www.butkus.org/information/worlds_fair_1934/world_fair_1934-1.pdf (*accessed August 31, 2015) 24.

36 *George's work*: Unsigned article, "Caldwells Leave Friday to Make Cleveland Home," *The Courier-Crescent*, April 2, 1942, 1.

36 *Ellen as a cook*: Charles Caldwell, interviews with the author.

37 *Doing dishes:* Charles Caldwell, interviews with the author.

38 *Delivering newspapers*: Charles Caldwell, interviews with the author.

39 *Getting a bicycle*: Charles Caldwell, interviews with the author.

40 *Big expectations*: Charles Caldwell, interviews with the author.

40 *Orrville High School*: Charles Caldwell, interviews with the author.

40 *Church addition*: Witmer, *Orrville, Ohio, Historical Walking Guide,* 15-6.

40 *Boarders*: Charles Caldwell, interviews with the author.

41 *Wayne County Hobby Exposition*: Unsigned article, "Thousand Persons See Hobby Exhibits in First County Show," *The Courier-Crescent*, April 3, 2015, 1.

41 *Hobby Exposition winners*: Unsigned article, "Thousand Persons See Hobby Exhibits in First County Show," April 3, 2015.

42 *Gone With the Wind display in store*: Charles Caldwell, interviews with the author.

44 *Grandfather dies*: Unsigned article, "Father of Rev. Caldwell Dies Thursday in Florida," *The Courier-Crescent*, April 8, 1940, 1.

45 *Wayne County Hobby Exposition*: Unsigned article, "Charles Caldwell's Clay Models Win Hobby Prize," *The Courier-Crescent*, May 20, 1940, 1.

45 *Getting driver's license*: Charles Caldwell, interviews with the author.

46 *Band dates*: Charles Caldwell, interviews with the author.

46 *Century Wood Preserving Plant*: Roger Scott, "Remember Koppers Wood Preserving plant?" *The Courier-Crescent*, June 17, 2011, 19; Charles Caldwell, interviews with the author.

48 *Tea compresses:* Charles Caldwell, interviews with the author.
49 *Murder at plant*: Charles Caldwell, interviews with the author.
49 *Getting in University of Alabama*: Unsigned article, "Charles Caldwell Finds His Dream Is True," *The Courier-Crescent*, September 15, 1941, 1.

Becoming a Marine

50 *William G. Little*: Winton Groom, *The Crimson Tide: An Illustrated History of Football at The University of Alabama* (Tuscaloosa, AL: The University of Alabama Press, 2000), 4.
50 *University of Alabama football history*: Groom, *The Crimson Tide,* 4, 8.
51 *Only college applied to*: Charles Caldwell, interviews with the author.
51 *Last day at Century Wood Preserving*: Charles Caldwell, interviews with the author.
51 *Arriving at University of Alabama*: Charles Caldwell, interviews with the author.
52 *Freshman dormitories*: Robert Oliver Mellown, *The University of Alabama: A Guide to the Campus and Its Architecture* (Tuscaloosa, AL: The University of Alabama Press, 2013), 117.
52 *Origin of Crimson Tide*: Groom, *The Crimson Tide,* 17.
53 *Tackling dummy*: Charles Caldwell, interviews with the author.
53 *Picked on*: Charles Caldwell, interviews with the author.
53 *Size of linemen*: Cork Gaines, "NFL Linemen Weren't Always Big and Fat – See How Much They've Grown Over the Years," Business Insider, *http://www.businessinsider.com/nfl-50s-tim-tebow-would-have-been-an-offensive-lineman-2011-10?op=1#ixzz3gknbI1QJ* (accessed September 2, 2015).
54 *Work and classes*: Charles Caldwell, interviews with the author.
54 *Failing classes*: Charles Caldwell, interviews with the author.
55 Pearl Harbor attack: Charles Caldwell, interviews with the author.
56 *Pearl Harbor casualties*: "Pearl Harbor," World War 2 History, *http://www.worldwar2history.info/Pearl-Harbor* (accessed September 2, 2015).
57 *Roosevelt's address*: "Day of Infamy Franklin D. Roosevelt – December 7, 1941," RadioChemistry.org, *http://www.radiochemistry.org/history/nuclear_age/06_fdr_infamy.shtml* (accessed September 2, 2015).
58 *Marine enlistment requirements*: A display at the Parris Island Museum in Beaufort, SC 29902-7607.
58 *Chuck joins Marines*: Charles Caldwell, interviews with the author.
59 *Final physical*: Charles Caldwell, interviews with the author.

60 *First local man to enlist*: Unsigned article, "Here's Review of Events That Made News in the Last Half of 1941," *The Crescent-Courier*, January 5, 1942, 1.

60 *Leaving Cleveland*: Charles Caldwell, interviews with the author.

60 *Behavior on the train*: "Memorandum to All Recruits," Undated memorandum issued from United States Marine Corps Headquarters, Recruiting District of Cleveland, 520-524 Federal Building, Public Square, Cleveland, Ohio, from Charles Caldwell's memorabilia.

61 *Frank Sloza*: Charles Caldwell, interviews with the author.

61 *Breakfast*: Postcard from Chuck Caldwell to his parents, December 31, 1941.

62 *Yemassee*: "Town of Yemassee," Town of Yemassee, *http://townofyemassee.org/* (accessed September 2, 2015).

62 *Arrival in Yemassee*: A display at the Parris Island Museum in Beaufort, SC 29902-7607.

63 *Parris Island*: Eugene Alvarez, *Parris Island: Once a Recruit, Always a Marine* (Charleston, SC: History Press, 2013), 16; Ed Evans, "Parris Island," *Leatherneck*, December 1969, 27.

63 *"Called things I'd never even heard before"*: Charles Caldwell, interviews with the author.

63 *Parris Island induction*: Robert Leckie, *Helmet for my Pillow* (New York: Random House, 2011), 7; Charles Caldwell, interviews with the author.

64 *Wake Island:* Charles Caldwell, interviews with the author.

65 *Japanese toymakers*: Charles Caldwell, interviews with the author.

65 *Acting Jacks:* Alvarez, *Parris Island,* 21-22.

66 *In trouble with drill instructor*: Charles Caldwell, interviews with the author.

66 *Qualifying on the range*: Alvarez, *Parris Island,* 21-22.

67 *Food on the range*: Charles Caldwell, interviews with the author.

67 *Mess sergeant busted*: Charles Caldwell, interviews with the author.

67 *Inoculations*: Leckie, *Helmet for my Pillow,* 13-14.

67 *Anthony J. Drexel Biddle*: James N. Wright, "On the Art of Hand to Hand: An Interview with Col. A. J. Drexel Biddle, USMCR, *http://homepage.ntlworld.com/jimmy_fatwing/Military/biddle.htm* (accessed September 2, 2015); Joseph R. Svinth, "Anthony J. Drexel Biddle, USMC CQB Pioneer," ejmas.com, *http://ejmas.com/jnc/jncart_Svinth_1201.htm* (accessed September 2, 2015).

69 *Part of history:* Charles Caldwell, interviews with the author.

Entering the War

70 *Chuck's opinion of the Bloemfontein*: Charles Caldwell, interviews with the author.

70 *Bloemfontein as a cruise ship*: *Bloemfontein*, a brochure about the ship that Chuck Caldwell has in his memorabilia collection. There is no date or publishing information on Chuck's copy.

70 *Army takes over Bloemfontein*: Jacques Jansen van Vuuren, "M. S. Bloemfontein," Pacific War 1941-1945, May 25, 2009, http://www.network54.com/Forum/594514/thread/1243241775/M.+S.+Bloemfontein (accessed September 25, 2015).

72 *"...dust tickled their noses"*: John M. Hennessey, *...The difference: A History of the 5th and 14th Defense Battalions United States Marine Corps* (Privately published, 1989), 30.

72 *Sleeping on the ship:* Charles Caldwell, interviews with the author.

73 *Life aboard the ship*: Charles Caldwell, interviews with the author.

74 *Filling holes in the units*: Charles Caldwell, interviews with the author.

75 *Food aboard the ship*: Charles Caldwell, interviews with the author.

75 *"...squatted over ship's rails":* Hennessey, *The difference*, 32.

76 *Practical jokes*: Charles Caldwell, interviews with the author.

76 *Elmer Eaton*: Charles Caldwell, interviews with the author.

77 *Francis Marion Ashcroft*: Company records that Chuck Caldwell has in his personal collection.

77 *Entering the canal:* Charles Caldwell, interviews with the author.

77 *Cost of the canal:* Lee Krystek, "Connecting the Pacific and the Atlantic: The Panama Canal", The Museum of Unnatural History, 2011, *http://www.unmuseum.org/7wonders/panama_canal.htm* (accessed September 25, 2105).

78 *Moving through the canal*: "Panama Canal facts in brief," ErinBernhardt.net.nz, March 13, 2015, http://erwin.bernhardt.net.nz/america/panamacanalfacts.html (accessed September 25, 2015).

79 *Barrage balloons*: Charles Caldwell, interviews with the author.

80 *Equator crossing ceremony*: "Panama Canal facts in brief," ErinBernhardt.net.nz; Charles Caldwell, interviews with the author.

81 *Arriving at Wellington*: Charles Caldwell, interviews with the author.

82 *Liberty in Wellington*: Hennessey, *...The difference,* 33.

83 *Fifth Defense Battalion history*: Laura Wood, "5th and 14th Marine Defense Battalions Memorial," War Memorials HQ, 2011, *http://www.warmemorialhq.org/cpg/displayimage.php?album=567&pid=3743#top_display_media* (accessed September 25, 2015).

83 *Steak and eggs*: Charles Caldwell, interviews with the author.

83 *Travels in the Pacific*: Charles Caldwell, interviews with the author; Robert F. Dorr, "Unsung battle: Fighting at Funafuti Atoll played an important role in World War II", Leatherneck Magazine, June 21, 2004, *http://www.leatherneck.com/forums/showthread.php?15213-Unsung-battle-Fighting-at-Funafuti-Atoll-played-an-important-role-in-World-War-II* (accessed September 25, 2015).

86 *Eddie Rickenbacker*: Billy A. Rea, "Eddie Rickenbacker and Six Other People Survive a B-17 Crash and Three Weeks Lost in the Pacific Ocean", HistoryNet, June 12, 2006, *http://www.historynet.com/eddie-rickenbacker-and-six-other-people-survive-a-b-17-crash-and-three-weeks-lost-in-the-pacific-ocean.htm* (access September 25, 2015).

88 *Ellice natives*: October 3, 1942, Chuck Caldwell's diary that he kept during his time around the Battle of Guadalcanal.

88 *Carrying shells*: October 4, 1942, Chuck Caldwell's Guadalcanal diary.

89 *Liberty*: Charles Caldwell, interviews with the author.

Guadalcanal

90 *Guadalcanal description*: Donald L. Miller, *D-Days in the Pacific*, (New York: Simon & Schuster, 2005), 48.

90 *Size of invasion*: Patrick O'Donnell, "The Marines on Guadalcanal," World War 2 History Info, 2002, *http://www.worldwar2history.info/Guadalcanal/Marines.html* (accessed October 3, 2015).

91 *Surprise attack*: O'Donnell, "The Marines on Guadalcanal," World War 2 History Info.

91 *Admiral Fletcher replaced*: Barrett Tillman, "William Bull Halsey: Legendary World War II Admiral," Historynet, June 7, 2007, *http://www.historynet.com/william-bull-halsey-legendary-world-war-ii-admiral.htm* (accessed October 3, 2015).

92 *Second raid*: O'Donnell, "The Marines on Guadalcanal," World War 2 History Info.

92 *2,000 Japanese soldiers attack*: O'Donnell, "The Marines on Guadalcanal," World War 2 History Info.

92 *Marines pull back*: O'Donnell, "The Marines on Guadalcanal," World War 2 History Info.

93 *Kawaguchi attacks*: O'Donnell, "The Marines on Guadalcanal," World War 2 History Info.

93 *Half the Raiders killed*: O'Donnell, "The Marines on Guadalcanal," World War 2 History Info.

93 *USS Libra's guns*: "USS Libra (LKA-12) ex USS Libra (AKA-12) (1943-1969) USS Libra (AK-53) (1942-1943)," NavSource Online:

Amphibious Photo Archive, April 12, 2013, *http://www.navsource.org/archives/10/02/02012.htm* (accessed October 3, 2015).

93 *November 2 attack*: Miller, *D-Days in the Pacific*, 49.

95 *Day's worth of ammunition*: Jim McEnery, *Hell in the Pacific: A Marine rifleman's journey from Guadalcanal Canal to Peleliu* (New York: Simon & Schuster, 2012), 9.

95 *Coming ashore*: Charles Caldwell, interviews with the author.

96 *Push to Henderson Field*: Charles Caldwell, interviews with the author.

97 *Japanese in camp*: Charles Caldwell, interviews with the author.

98 *Visit cemetery*: Charles Caldwell, interviews with the author; "Burial of dead Marines at a cemetery in Guadalcanal, Solomon Islands during World War II," Critical Past, 2015, *http://www.criticalpast.com/video/65675044978_United-States-Marines_priests-at-altar_grave-covered-with-palm-leaves_cemetery* (accessed October 8, 2015)

98 *Swimming and washing*: Charles Caldwell, interviews with the author.

98 *George Noll*: Charles Caldwell, interviews with the author.

99 *November 12 air raid*: Charles Caldwell, interviews with the author.

100 *Coconut trees falling*: Charles Caldwell, interviews with the author.

100 *Chuck wounded*: Charles Caldwell, interviews with the author.

101 *"Had I stayed where I was":* Charles Caldwell, interviews with the author.

101 *Mosquitoes:* Charles Caldwell, interviews with the author.

101 *George Noll attacked by mosquitoes*: Charles Caldwell, interviews with the author.

101 *Battle of Savo Island*: David H. Lippman, "Battle of Guadalcanal: First Naval Battle in the Ironbottom Sound," HistoryNet, June 12, 2006, *http://www.historynet.com/battle-of-guadalcanal-first-naval-battle-in-the-ironbottom-sound.htm* (accessed October 8, 2015); Donald L. Miller, Henry Steele Commager, *The Story of World War II* (New York: Simon and Schuster, 2001), 134-5.

103 *Japanese wounded on beach*: Charles Caldwell, interviews with the author.

104 *Chuck marks graves*: Charles Caldwell, interviews with the author.

104 *Harp McGuire*: Charles Caldwell, interviews with the author; "Harp McGuire (1921-1966)," Imdb.com, *http://www.imdb.com/name/nm0570205/?ref_=fn_al_nm_1* (accessed October 8, 2015).

104 *Washing Machine Charlie*: Charles Caldwell, interviews with the author.

105 *Dysentery and malaria*: McEnery, *Hell in the Pacific,* 132.

105 *General Patch takes command*: Charles Caldwell, interviews with the author; McEnery, *Hell in the Pacific,* 135.
105 *Interrupting Patch and Vandergrift*: Charles Caldwell, interviews with the author.
106 *Headhunters*: Charles Caldwell, interviews with the author.
107 *Beheaded nuns*: Charles Caldwell, interviews with the author.
107 *Wiping out a village*: Charles Caldwell, interviews with the author.
107 *Zale Rains*: Charles Caldwell, interviews with the author; December 21, 22, 1942, Chuck Caldwell's Guadalcanal diary.
108 *Ketchup:* December 25, 1942, Chuck Caldwell's Guadalcanal diary.
108 *Solomon Islands secure*: December 30, 1942, Chuck Caldwell's Guadalcanal diary.
109 *Bomb almost in camp*: January 15, 1943, Chuck Caldwell's Guadalcanal diary.
109 *Five Marines killed*: January 15, 1943, Chuck Caldwell's Guadalcanal diary.
109 *Bold Japanese*: January 27, 1943, Chuck Caldwell's Guadalcanal diary.
110 *Eaton's promotion*: Charles Caldwell, interviews with the author.
111 February storm: February 24, 1943, Chuck Caldwell's Guadalcanal diary.
112 *Recreation:* March 13, 1943, Chuck Caldwell's Guadalcanal diary.
112 *Radio Tokyo:* March 19, 1943, Chuck Caldwell's Guadalcanal diary.
112 *Presidential citation*: March 22, 1943, Chuck Caldwell's Guadalcanal diary.
113 *Trading souvenirs*: March 23, 1943, Chuck Caldwell's Guadalcanal diary.
113 *Going to Tulagi*: March 25 & 28, 1943, Chuck Caldwell's Guadalcanal diary.

Tarawa

115 *Going to Tulagi*: Charles Caldwell, interviews with the author.
115 *Tulagi description*: Hennessey, *...The difference*, 40-1.
116 *Tulagi invasion*: Miller, *D-Days in the Pacific,* 50.
116 *Naval base and refueling station*: Stanley Coleman Jersey, *Hell's Islands: The Untold Story of Guadalcanal* (College Station, TX: Texas A&M University Press, 2008), 3; Samuel B. Griffith, *Battle for Guadalcanal* (Champaign, IL: University of Illinois Press, 1963), 93.
116 *P.T. Boats*: Hennessey, *...The difference*, 45, 58.
116 *All hills*: Charles Caldwell, interviews with the author.
116 *April 7 attack*: "Col. James Swett - Pilot / Triple Ace, VMF-221, VMF-141, Congressional Medal of Honor - An American Hero," High Iron Illustrations,

http://www.highironillustrations.com/rogues/james_swett.html (accessed December 21, 2015); Charles Caldwell, interviews with the author.

117 *James Swett*: Stephen Sherman, "Marine Corps Aces of WWII: Wildcat and Corsair pilots at Guadalcanal and the Solomons," AcePilots.com, http://acepilots.com/usmc_aces.html#Swett (accessed December 21, 2015); Charles Caldwell, interviews with the author.

117 *Chuck shooting down dive bomber*: Charles Caldwell, interviews with the author.

118 *Chuck burning his hands*: Charles Caldwell, interviews with the author.

118 *Leaving Tulagi*: Hennessey, …The difference, 132.

119 *Only part of Fifth Battalion that saw combat*: Charles Caldwell, interviews with the author.

119 *Part of Second Division:* Charles Caldwell, interviews with the author.

120 *"Most-misguided outfit":* Charles Caldwell, interviews with the author.

121 *Admiral Hill's message*: Capt. Earl J. Wilson and Marine Combat Correspondents Master Technical Sergeants Jim G. Lucas (now 2nd Lt.) and Samuel Shaffer, and Staff Sergeant C. Peter Zurlinden (now 2nd Lt.), *Betio Beachhead: U.S. Marines' Own Story of The Battle for Tarawa* (New York: G. P. Putnam's Sons, 1945), 16.

121 *Betio Island:* Wilson, Lucas, Shaffer, and Zurlinden, *Betio Beachhead,* 16.

121 *Japanese fortifications*: Derrick Wright, *Tarawa 1943: The Turning of the Tide* (Oxford, England: Osprey Publishing, 2010), 10.

122 *American invasion force:* "The Battle of Tarawa," Wikipedia, http://en.wikipedia.org/wiki/Battle_of_Tarawa (accessed December 21, 2015).

122 *What Marines did at sea*: Wilson, Lucas, Shaffer, and Zurlinden, *Betio Beachhead,* 20, 22.

122 *Arrival at Betio:* Wilson, Lucas, Shaffer, and Zurlinden, *Betio Beachhead,* 25.

123 *Clearing mines*: Richard Wheeler, *A Special Valor : the U.S. Marines and the Pacific War* (New York: Harper & Row, 1983), 174.

123 *First casualty*: Wilson, Lucas, Shaffer, and Zurlinden, *Betio Beachhead,* 32.

124 *Climbing into Higgins boat*: Miller, D-*Days in the Pacific,* 63-4.

125 *First waves of boats get stuck*: Wilson, Lucas, Shaffer, and Zurlinden, *Betio Beachhead,* 38; Charles Caldwell, interviews with the author.

125 *Water too deep*: Wilson, Lucas, Shaffer, and Zurlinden, *Betio Beachhead,* 44.

125 *Scavenging ammunition belts*: Wilson, Lucas, Shaffer, and Zurlinden,

Betio Beachhead, 58.

126 *300 dead*: Charles Caldwell, interviews with the author.

126 *Swam underwater*: Charles Caldwell, interviews with the author.

127 *Establishing a beachhead*: Wilson, Lucas, Shaffer, and Zurlinden, *Betio Beachhead,* 52.

129 *Caught in a crossfire*: Wilson, Lucas, Shaffer, and Zurlinden, *Betio Beachhead,* 68.

129 *Night dangers on pier*: Wilson, Lucas, Shaffer, and Zurlinden, *Betio Beachhead,* 68.

130 *Sinking Liscome Bay*: USS Liscome Bay (CVE 56), Navysite.de, *http://www.navysite.de/cve/cve56.htm* (accessed December 21, 2015).

130 *Holes in pants*: Charles Caldwell, interviews with the author.

Recovery

132 *Chuck summarizes Tarawa*: Charles Caldwell, interviews with the author.

132 *Tarawa casualties*: "Casualties," Tarawa on the Web, *http://www.tarawaontheweb.org/casualty.htm* (accessed January 26, 2016).

133 *Marines build camp*: Charles Caldwell, interviews with the author.

133 *MOB4*: Charles Caldwell, interviews with the author; Lt. Col. Eugene T. Lyons, MSC, "Part V The Pacific, Chapter XV Australia and New Zealand, Section I. Australia," U. S. Army Medical Department Office of Medical History, *http://history.amedd.army.mil/booksdocs/wwii/civilaffairs/chapter15.htm* (accessed January 26, 2016); Joseph L. Schwartz, Captain (MC) USN (Retired), "Chapter I: Facilities of the Medical Department of the Navy, Continental and Extracontinental Hospitals," History of the Medical Department of the United States Navy in World War II, *http://www.ibiblio.org/hyperwar/USN/USN-Medical/I/USN-Medical-1.html* (accessed January 26, 2016).

134 *Angel of Mercy:* Charles Caldwell, interviews with the author.

136 *Chuck goes to Guam*: Charles Caldwell, interviews with the author.

136 *Hit by weak bullet*: Charles Caldwell, interviews with the author.

136 *Steps in body*: Charles Caldwell, interviews with the author.

137 *Cut cards:* Charles Caldwell, interviews with the author.

137 *Chuck heads home*: Charles Caldwell, interviews with the author.

137 *Date with usherettes:* Charles Caldwell, interviews with the author.

138 *Finds out Glenn Miller died*: Charles Caldwell, interviews with the author.

138 *Train ride to Cleveland*: Charles Caldwell, interviews with the author.

140 *Parents don't recognize Chuck*: Charles Caldwell, interviews with the author.

140 *Move to Cleveland*: Unsigned article, "Caldwells Leave Friday to Make Cleveland Home," *The Courier-Crescent*, April 2, 1942, 1.

141 *Barbara's husband*: Charles Caldwell, interviews with the author.

141 *Civil War rifle*: Charles Caldwell, interviews with the author.

143 *Mom leaves him whiskey*: Charles Caldwell, interviews with the author.

A War Ends, A Marriage Begins

144 *WAVES:* C. Peter Chen, "WAVES: Women in the WW2 US Navy," WWII Database, *ww2db.com/other.php?other_id=24* (accessed February 15, 2016).

144 *Allerton Hotel:* E. J. Imhof, "The Allerton Hotel," The Cleveland Memory Project, Michael Schwartz Library at Michigan State University, *imag-
es.ulib.csuohio.edu/cdm/singleitem/collection/postcards/id/1948/rec/1* (accessed February 15, 2016); Michael DeAloia, "The Allerton Hotel," Cool History of Cleveland, *coolhistoryofcleve-
land.wordpress.com/2011/02/20/the-allerton-hotel* (accessed February 15, 2016).

144 *Meeting Jackie*: Charles Caldwell, interviews with the author.

145 *Angel of Mercy*: Charles Caldwell, interviews with the author.

146 *Asking Jackie out*: Charles Caldwell, interviews with the author.

146 *Dating:* Charles Caldwell, interviews with the author.

147 *About Jackie*: Unsigned article, "Charles Caldwell to Wed Youngstown Lass," *The Courier-Crescent*, April 5, 1945, 4.

148 *Getting engaged*: Charles Caldwell, interviews with the author.

148 *Duties at Parris Island*: Charles Caldwell, interviews with the author.

149 *Marriage:* Charles Caldwell, interviews with the author.

151 *Discharged*: Charles Caldwell, interviews with the author.

151 Telling & Belle Vernon Dairy job: Charles Caldwell, interviews with the author.

152 *Postal inspection job*: Charles Caldwell, interviews with the author.

152 *1,000 Myflam lighters*: Charles Caldwell, interviews with the author.

154 *Returning to college*: Charles Caldwell, interviews with the author.

154 *Not getting housing*: Charles Caldwell, interviews with the author; *University of Alabama Bulletin Catalogue Issue 1948-49 with Announcements for 1949-50* (Tuscaloosa, AL: University of Alabama) 421.

155 *Chuck's college plan*: Charles Caldwell, interviews with the author.

155 *Pledging fraternity*: Charles Caldwell, interviews with the author; Unsigned article, "7 Students Initiated By Art Fraternity," from unknown

newspaper in scrapbook owned by Charles Caldwell, undated article.
156 *Jackie loses baby*: Charles Caldwell, interviews with the author.
156 *Moundville*: John H. Blitz, "Moundville Archaeological Park," Encyclopedia of Alabama, *www.encyclopediaofalabama.org/article/h-1045* (accessed February 15, 2016).
158 *Job at Oak Ridge*: Charles Caldwell, interviews with the author.
159 *Accelerating classes*: Charles Caldwell, interviews with the author.
159 *Graduating college:* Charles Caldwell, interviews with the author.

Mushroom Clouds

160 *Clinton Engineer Works*: Lindsey A. Freeman, *Longing for the Bomb: Oak Ridge and Atomic Nostalgia* (Chapel Hill, NC: The University of North Carolina Press, 2015), xiii.
160 *Displaced three times*: Denise Kiernan, *The Girls of Atomic City: The Untold Story of the Women Who Helped Win World War II* (New York: Simon & Schuster, 2013), 23.
161 *Football jerseys*: Freeman, *Longing for the Bomb*, 3.
162 *Ghost Towns:* Freeman, *Longing for the Bomb*, 105-6.
162 *Seeking incorporation*: Freeman, *Longing for the Bomb*, 109.
162 *Vote against incorporation*: William K. Wilcox Jr., "The Day They Opened The Gates of The Secret City: A Research Paper Prepared for the 60th Anniversary of the Opening of the Secret City Gates," Bill Wilcox Historical Articles Collection, Oak Ridge Historical and Preservation Association, 2009, *http://www.oakridgeheritage.com/orhpa-archives/bill-wilcox-historical-articles-collection* (accessed March 4, 2016), 2.
162 *Advantages of closed community* Freeman, *Longing for the Bomb*, 113.
163 *Gate opening*: Freeman, *Longing for the Bomb*, 114.
163 *Opening of Atomic Energy Museum*: Freeman, *Longing for the Bomb*, 121.
163 *Museum mission*: Wilcox, "The Day They Opened The Gates of The Secret City," 12.
164 *Admission to museum*: Wilcox, "The Day They Opened The Gates of The Secret City," 12.
164 *Raising prices because of mud:* Charles Caldwell, interviews with the author.
165 *Irradiated dimes*: A million dimes were irradiated from 1949 to 1967 before the metal composition of the coin was changed so that it could no longer hold the radioactive charge. Freeman, *Longing for the Bomb*, 124.
165 *Radioactive turtles* Freeman, *Longing for the Bomb*, 124.

166 *Problems at the museum:* Charles Caldwell, interviews with the author.
166 *Reactivated for war:* Charles Caldwell, interviews with the author.
167 *Going home for weekends*: Charles Caldwell, interviews with the author.
168 *Near accident:* Charles Caldwell, interviews with the author.
168 *Switching jobs:* Charles Caldwell, interviews with the author.
168 *Parents' divorce:* Charles Caldwell, interviews with the author.
169 *Cemesto:* Charles Caldwell, interviews with the author.
171 Spotsylvania re-enactment: Bill Felknor, "Civil War Enthusiast Rebuilds Confederacy," *The Oak Ridger*, March 5, 1965, clipping in Chuck Caldwell scrapbook.
171 *John Salling:* Charles Caldwell, interviews with the author; Anne Morse, "Fake War Stories Exposed," CBS News, November 11, 2005, *http://www.cbsnews.com/news/fake-war-stories-exposed/* (accessed March 4, 2016).
172 *Pleasant Crump:* Kitty Walker Lennard, "COL Pleasant 'Riggs' Crump," Find A Grave, *http://www.findagrave.com/cgi-bin/fg.cgi?page=gr&GRid=13397843* (accessed March 4, 2016).
172 *Albert Woolson:* Unsigned article, "Woolson, Last Union Veteran, Is Buried After Military Rites," *The New York Times*, August 7, 1956, 27; Unsigned article, "Last 24 Hours," *St. Petersburg Times*, August 3, 1956, 2.
173 *Volunteering for Nevada*: Charles Caldwell, interviews with the author.
173 *Selecting Nevada Test Site*: Michon Mackedon, *Bombast: Spinning Atoms in the Desert* (Reno, NV: Black Rock Institute Press, 2010), xi, 1.
174 *Fallout zones:* Mackedon, *Bombast*, 29.
174 *Explosion description:* Mackedon, *Bombast*, 34.
174 *Routine testing:* Mackedon, *Bombast*, 35.
175 *"Excited to be there":* Charles Caldwell, interviews with the author.
176 *Wendell Ogg*: B. J. Corbin, "1949 A.J. Smith, College Dean," *The Explorers Of Ararat: And the Search for Noah's Ark - 3rd Edition*, Online Version, NoahsArkSearch.com, http://www.noahsarksearch.com/explorers_of_ararat_3rd_edition.htm (accessed March 4, 2016), 223.
176 *Test site homes*: Charles Caldwell, interviews with the author.
176 *Fission balls*: Charles Caldwell, interviews with the author.
177 *Concussive force doughnut*: Charles Caldwell, interviews with the author.
177 *Photographer gets knocked over:* Charles Caldwell, interviews with the author.

178 *Column still rising*: Charles Caldwell, interviews with the author.
179 *Operation Plumbbob:* "Operation Plumbbob – 1957," Atomic Heritage Foundation, *http://www.atomicheritage.org/history/operation-plumbbob-1957* (accessed March 4, 2016); Declassified documents show that the Plumbbob test series released approximately 58,300 kilocuries of radioiodine (I-131) into the atmosphere over four months. This produced 120 million person-rads of thyroid tissue exposure for civilians. Three thousand soldiers were also exposed to high levels of radiation during exercises near the ground near the Smoky test detonation. A 1980 survey showed that these men had significantly elevated rates of leukemia.
179 *Hood Test:* "Operation Plumbbob: 1957 - Nevada Test Site," *The Nuclear Weapon Archive.*
179 *Radiation suits:* Charles Caldwell, interviews with the author.
180 *Going in after Hood:* Charles Caldwell, interviews with the author.
181 *Taking David to detonation*: Charles Caldwell, interviews with the author.
182 Building Disneyland: "Disneyland's History," JustDisney.com, *http://www.justdisney.com/disneyland/history.html* (accessed March 4, 2016).
182 *Meeting Walt Disney:* Charles Caldwell, interviews with the author.
183 *Jackie loses child:* Charles Caldwell, interviews with the author.
184 *Operation Hardtack II*: "Operation Hardtack II: 1958 - Nevada Test Site," Atomic Heritage Foundation, *http://nuclearweaponarchive.org/Usa/Tests/Hardtack2.html* (accessed March 4, 2016).

A Fake War

185 *Children's birth:* Charles Caldwell, interviews with the author; David Caldwell, interview with the author, November 23, 2015.
185 *Old guard houses*: David Caldwell, interview with the author.
186 *Warning horn*: David Caldwell, interview with the author.
186 *Open house*: Unsigned article, "Reactor Monument Open Thursday," newspaper clipping in Chuck Caldwell's scrapbook, August 28, 1968; David Caldwell, interview with the author.
186 *Wandering in woods*: Freeman, *Longing for the Bomb*, 106.
186 *Foxfire glow*: David Caldwell, interview with the author.
187 *Joining a church*: Charles Caldwell, interviews with the author.
187 *Treehouses*: Charles Caldwell, interviews with the author.
188 *East Tennessee winters*: David Caldwell, interview with the author.
188 *Pets around the house*: Charles Caldwell, interviews with the author.

189 *Shiloh re-enactment*: "1st Tennessee Infantry Regiment (Provisional Army)," The Civil War in the East, *http://civilwarintheeast.com/CSA/TN/1TN.php* (accessed March 4, 2016).

189 *Forming re-enacting company*: Charles Caldwell, interviews with the author.

190 *Turney footlocker*: Felknor, "Civil War Enthusiast Rebuilds Confederacy," March 5, 1965.

190 *Finding Isaac Caldwell*: Charles Caldwell, interviews with the author; Judy Henley Phillips, "Peter Turney's 1st Tennessee Regiment Company C," The Civil War in Franklin County, Tennessee, November 28, 2004, *http://www.tngenweb.org/franklin/franc.htm#C* (accessed March 4, 2016). There is some discrepancy with Caldwell's description. On the oath of Allegiance he took at Point Lookout, Md., on June 24, 1865, he is listed as being from Franklin County with a dark complexion, black hair, light hazel eyes and standing five feet eleven and a quarter inches tall. It is believed that the latter is correct and the former applies to a deserter named J. C. Caldwell.

190 *Chuck re-enacting:* Felknor, "Civil War Enthusiast Rebuilds Confederacy," March 5, 1965.

191 *No veterans at 100th anniversary*: Charles Caldwell, interviews with the author.

192 *POW camp*: Unsigned article, "Tells How War Prisoners Are Treated Here," *The Gettysburg Times*, July 14, 1944, 4.

192 *Re-enactors' uniforms*: Charles Caldwell, interviews with the author.

192 *Re-enactors' parade:* Unsigned article, "Crowd Of More Than 35,000 View Centennial Parade On Tuesday; Rain Delays Start," *The Gettysburg Times*, July 2, 1963, 1.

193 *Heckler in crowd:* Charles Caldwell, interviews with the author.

193 *Pickett's Charge re-enactment:* Unsigned article, "Colorful Re-enactment of Pickett's Charge Attracts Huge Crowd," *The Gettysburg Times*, July 5, 1963, 1.

193 *Re-enactors wear sunglasses*: Unsigned article, "Colorful Re-enactment of Pickett's Charge Attracts Huge Crowd," July 5, 1963.

194 *Jackie thinks Burns is Johnny Appleseed*: Charles Caldwell, interviews with the author.

194 *Jackie turned off re-enacting*: Charles Caldwell, interviews with the author.

194 *Appomattox march*: Felknor, "Civil War Enthusiast Rebuilds Confederacy," March 5, 1965.

195 *Foothills Craft Guild*: "History & Heritage," Foothills Craft Guild,

http://foothillscraftguild.org/guild-history-heritage (accessed March 4, 2016).

195 *Sculpey:* Dot Decamp, "Charles Caldwell Display of Baseball Models At Library During March," unknown newspaper clipping in Charles Caldwell's scrapbook, March 20, 1969; Charles Caldwell, interviews with the author; Fred Stewart, "Hobby? Future?," *The Oak Ridger*, no date, clipping from Chuck Caldwell's scrapbook.

195 *100 Figures in a month:* Charles Caldwell, interviews with the author.

196 *Sculpey test:* Fred Stewart, "Hobby? Future?," no date.

197 *Chuck quits ORNL:* Willard Yarbrough, "Oak Ridger Makes Hit as Sculptor," *The Knoxville News-Sentinel*, December 22, 1968, clipping from Chuck Caldwell's scrapbook; Charles Caldwell, interviews with the author.

197 "…a gift of God": Willard Yarbrough, "Oak Ridger Makes Hit as Sculptor," December 22, 1968.

198 *Trip through downtown D.C.*: Charles Caldwell, interviews with the author.

198 *Washington D.C. riots*: Rob Brent, "Riots Erupt in Washington, DC Following Martin Luther King, Jr. Assassination," World History Project, *https://worldhistoryproject.org/1968/4/4/riots-erupt-in-washington-dc-following-martin-luther-king-jr-assassination* (accessed March 4, 2016); Charles Caldwell, interviews with the author.

199 *Riot damage:* Rob Brent, "Riots Erupt in Washington, DC Following Martin Luther King, Jr. Assassination," World History Project; "CPI Inflation Calculator," *Bureau of Labor Statistics*, Department of Labor, *http://www.bls.gov/data/inflation_calculator.htm* (accessed March 4, 2015).

199 *Hall of Presidents:* This is an ongoing assignment for Chuck. At the time, he created figures of all of the presidents up to Lyndon Johnson. Since then, he has made a new figure for each new president. Currently, he is up to Barack Obama. The figures are still on display in the Hall of Presidents in Gettysburg.; T. W. Burger and Jeffery B. Roth, "End of an Era in Gettysburg," *The Gettysburg Times,* November 27, 1987, 12a.

199 *Getting cocky*: Charles Caldwell, interviews with the author.

199 *Natural History Museum*: Yarbrough, "Oak Ridger Makes Hit as Sculptor," December 22, 1968.

199 *American Woodland Museum*: Unsigned article, "Rotary Club to tour new museum," *Oneonta Star*, May 14, 1962, 2; Harold H. Hollis, *The History of Cooperstown 1929-1975* (Cooperstown, NY: The New York State Historical Association, 1976), 349; Unsigned article, "Louis Busch Hager, 58, Theatrical Producer," *The New York Times*, Decem-

ber 18, 1988, http://www.nytimes.com/1988/12/18/obituaries/louis-busch-hager-58-theatrical-producer.html (accessed March 4, 2016).

200 *Cardinals figures*: Charles Caldwell, interviews with the author; Yarbrough, "Oak Ridger Makes Hit as Sculptor," December 22, 1968.

200 *Bob Gibson*: "Bob Gibson 1968 Game by Game Pitching Logs," Baseball Almanac, *http://www.baseball-almanac.com/players/pitchinglogs.php?p=gibsobo01&y=1968* (accessed March 4, 2016).

201 *One-man show*: Yarbrough, "Oak Ridger Makes Hit as Sculptor," December 22, 1968; "CPI Inflation Calculator," Bureau of Labor Statistics, Department of Labor.

201 *Success of trip*: Yarbrough, "Oak Ridger Makes Hit as Sculptor," December 22, 1968.

201 *Other assignments*: Unsigned article, "Sculpter Spurns Security, He Says Talent is Sacred," *Carrollton Chronicle*, August 7, 1974, 14.

201 *Tennessee Memorial*: Yarbrough, "Oak Ridger Makes Hit as Sculptor," December 22, 1968; "The State of Tennessee," Battle of Gettysburg, Stone Sentinels, *http://gettysburg.stonesentinels.com/confederate-monuments/confederate-state-monuments/tennessee/* (accessed March 4, 2016); Unsigned article, "Local sculptor leaving feted at 'Roast'," *The Oak Ridger*, May 14, 1974, 1.

202 *Jets and Browns*: Unsigned article, "Local sculptor leaving feted at 'Roast'," May 14, 1974.

202 *Atomic energy medals*: Unsigned Article, "Nixon Honors Atomic Pioneer Trio," *The Oak Ridger*, March 3, 1970, 1; Unsigned article, "Local sculptor leaving feted at 'Roast'," May 14, 1974.

203 *Quitting smoking*: Charles Caldwell, interviews with the author.

203 *LeRoy Smith*: Charles Caldwell, interviews with the author.

204 *David joins Marines:* David Caldwell, interview with the author; Charles Caldwell, interviews with the author.

205 *David at Parris Island:* David Caldwell, interview with the author.

205 *Yellow footprints:* Alvarez, *Parris Island*: *Once a Recruit. Always a Marine*, 44.

205 *Drill instructor yelling:* David Caldwell, interview with the author.

205 *Nearly sent to Vietnam*: David Caldwell, interview with the author.

206 *Interservice transfer:* David Caldwell, interview with the author.

206 *Chuck won't stay in Gettysburg*: Charles Caldwell, interviews with the author.

Lots of Clay Soldiers

207 *Dallas Show:* Charles Caldwell, interviews with the author.

207 *Howard Bros. Circus*: Deborah W. Walk, *The Circus in Miniature: The Howard Bros. Circus Model* (Sarasota, Fla.: Serbian Printing & Publishing, Inc., 2008), 59-60; Charles Caldwell, interviews with the author.
208 *Cowan sells store:* Charles Caldwell, interviews with the author.
208 *Looking for work:* Charles Caldwell, interviews with the author.
208 *Ring company*: Charles Caldwell, interviews with the author.
209 *Cleaning houses*: Charles Caldwell, interviews with the author.
209 *"Dark years":* Charles Caldwell, interviews with the author.
210 *Franklin Mint:* Charles Caldwell, interviews with the author; "About The Franklin Mint," *The Franklin Mint*. Facebook.com, *https://www.facebook.com/TheFranklinMintPage/info/?tab=page_info* (accessed March 3, 2016); U.S. Government, Department of the Census, *Household Money Income in 1975 and Selected Social and Economic Characteristics of Households ... Subject: Current Population Reports*, March 1977, Series P-60, No. 104, Washington, DC: Government Printing Office.
210 *Wants a pool:* Charles Caldwell, interviews with the author.
212 *Back to Gettysburg:* Charles Caldwell, interviews with the author.
213 *Chuck's parents die*: Charles Caldwell, interviews with the author.
214 *Re-enacting in Gettysburg movie*: Charles Caldwell, interviews with the author.
215 *Tom Berenger a customer*: Charles Caldwell, interviews with the author.
215 *Robert Caldwell in Navy*: Charles Caldwell, interviews with the author.
216 *Barbara dies*: Charles Caldwell, interviews with the author.
216 *Jackie dies*: Charles Caldwell, interviews with the author.

A Full Circle

220 *"Taking them to the grave":* Charles Caldwell, interviews with the author.
220 *Orrville High School reunion:* Charles Caldwell, interviews with the author.

ABOUT THE AUTHOR

James Rada, Jr. has written many works of historical fiction and non-fiction history. They include the popular books *Saving Shallmar: Christmas Spirit in a Coal Town, Canawlers* and *Battlefield Angels: The Daughters of Charity Work as Civil War Nurses.*

He lives in Gettysburg, Pa., where he works as a freelance writer. James has received numerous awards from the Maryland-Delaware-DC Press Association, Associated Press, Maryland State Teachers Association, Society of Professional Journalists, and Community Newspapers Holdings, Inc. for his newspaper writing.

If you would like to be kept up to date on new books being published by James or ask him questions, he can be reached by e-mail at *jimrada@yahoo.com.*

To see James' other books or to order copies on-line, go to *www.jamesrada.com.*

DON'T MISS THESE BOOKS BY JAMES RADA, JR.

BATTLEFIELD ANGELS: THE DAUGHTERS OF CHARITY WORK AS CIVIL WAR NURSES

The Daughters of Charity were the only trained nurses in the country at the start of the Civil War. Their services were so in demand that they were allowed to cross between the North and the South at the beginning of the war. The served on the battlefields, in hospitals, on riverboat hospitals, and in prisoner-of-war camps. Learn their stories of pioneering nursing to the wounded and dying on both sides of the war and how it improved nursing and broke down religious bias against Catholics in the U.S.

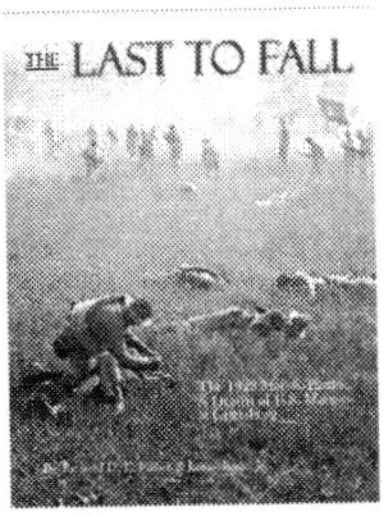

THE LAST TO FALL: THE 1922 MARCH, BATTLES, & DEATHS OF U.S. MARINES AT GETTYSBURG

In 1922, a quarter of the U.S. Marine Corps marched from Quantico, Va., to Gettysburg, Pa., where they conducted historical re-enactments of Pickett's Charge for 100,000 spectators, including the President of the United States. The Marines also conducted modern versions of the battle with tanks, machine guns and airplanes. Two Marines were killed on the battlefield during the exercises making them the last military line-of-duty deaths on the Gettysburg Battlefield.

NO NORTH, NO SOUTH...: THE GRAND REUNION AT THE 50TH ANNIVERSARY OF THE BATTLE OF GETTYSBURG

In 1913, more than 57,000 Civil War veterans returned to Gettysburg for the 50th anniversary of the battle fought there. Confederate and Union veterans alike spent a week on the battlefield reliving old memories and finally bringing peace between the North and the South.

Visit *www.jamesrada.com* for updates on author signings, presentations, & classes. You can also find out how to download three historical novels for FREE.

Available wherever books are sold.

32285234R00144

Made in the USA
Middletown, DE
29 May 2016